I THIRST

JACQUES GAUTHIER

I THIRST

Thérèse of Lisieux and Mother Teresa

A Striking Commonality
in the Spiritual Foundation of Saint Thérèse of Lisieux
and Blessed Mother Teresa of Calcutta

Translated by Alexandra Plettenberg-Serban

ST PAULS

Alba House

Originally published in French under the title *J'ai Soif: de la petite Thérèse à Mère Teresa* by Jacques Gauthier (Geneva: Parole et Silence, 2003).

Library of Congress Cataloging-in-Publication Data

Gauthier, Jacques, 1951-
  [J'ai soif. English]
  I thirst : Saint Thérèse of Lisieux and Mother Teresa of Calcutta / Jacques Gauthier ; translated by Alexandra Plettenberg-Serban.
    p. cm.
  Includes bibliographical references
  ISBN: 0-8189-0973-0
1. Thérèse, de Lisieux, Saint, 1873-1897. 2. Teresa, Mother, 1910-1997. I. Title.

  BX4700.T5G41313 2005
  282'.092'2—dc22

                                    2004024666

Produced and designed in the United States of America by the Fathers and Brothers of the Society of St. Paul, 2187 Victory Boulevard, Staten Island, New York 10314-6603, as part of their communications apostolate.

ISBN: 0-8189-0973-0

Printing Information:

Current Printing - first digit	1	2	3	4	5	6	7	8	9	10

Year of Current Printing - first year shown

2005	2006	2007	2008	2009	2010	2011	2012	2013	2014

St. Thérèse of Lisieux and Blessed Mother Teresa of Calcutta responded to the cry of Jesus on the Cross "I Thirst," finding the flow of love in the depth of His being, which they felt destined to share with all people.

"Unfortunately, [Jesus] finds few hearts who are committed to Him without reservation, and who understand the immense tenderness of His infinite love."

St. Thérèse of the Child Jesus, *Letter 196*
to Sister Marie of the Sacred Heart

"If you do not listen to Jesus in the silence of your own heart, you can not hear His voice in the heart of the poor saying, 'I thirst'.... You will miss Him if you do not go near Him. He thirsts for you."

Mother Teresa, *Spiritual Testament*

Table of Contents

Introduction to the English Version

This book which reveals the striking commonality in the spirituality of Saint Thérèse of Lisieux and Mother Teresa of Calcutta is something we have long been waiting for.

The author, Jacques Gauthier, Professor of Theology at St. Paul University Ottawa/Canada with over twenty-five books to his credit, grew over his lifetime into an ever deeper relationship with St. Thérèse of Lisieux, and dedicated four of his books to her. Today he is widely known in Canada and in France for his readings and teachings on radio and television.

His new study deals with two of the greatest women of their times and allows us to understand fully their spirituality, born in the depth of their hearts and yet firmly rooted in the Bible. We are shown how both women intuitively understood that the infinite desire of the Lord to love and to be loved by His people has its origin and source in the mystery of the thirst of Jesus. The author focuses on the immensely pragmatic nature of the faith of these two women. He shows how St. Thérèse and Mother Teresa went beyond the symbolism of the wounded heart of Jesus and His cry on the Cross in order to focus directly on the reality of Jesus Himself, His feelings, His love, His desire to be loved and His thirst for souls. Both women experienced His true presence in the heart of all people. In order to respond fully to their Lord's desire and thirst as their only mission, St. Thérèse ministered to Him in the most broken people around her, whereas Mother

Teresa found Jesus present in the hearts and faces of the poorest of the poor in the slums of Calcutta and the world. The spiritual closeness of Mother Teresa to St. Thérèse leads us to believe that St. Thérèse walked with Mother Teresa beyond the walls of her convent in Lisieux to the lame and the sick on the other side of the world, like two "working women," working out the greatest mystery of Christian spirituality. Their immense, all-consuming love that they as human beings were able to offer to others in whom they experienced Christ, flowed directly from the heart of Jesus Himself. Therefore Jacques Gauthier places the life of Mother Teresa among such Saints as Abraham, Elijah, Isaiah, Jeremiah, St. Francis of Assisi, St. Thérèse of Lisieux, and above all St. Paul. Gauthier makes it very clear that it is not our perfection that makes us builders of God's Kingdom on earth, but our "yes" in response to Jesus' thirst for love and sharing that love with others.

With the eyes of those two women, and the great men and women mystics before them, Jacques Gauthier takes us deep into the heart of Jesus and shares with us how Jesus, through His Sacred Wounds, invites us to partake in the divine dynamic of Trinitarian love. Like His disciples, we are asked to become brothers and sisters of Jesus, the divine Son of God, Who keeps His wounded heart open until the end of time, offering us a share in His overflowing love which causes the Spirit — Who eternally wants to share love — to be born in us.

I wish to express my gratitude to Dr. Frances Renda, who dedicated many hours to this work with her great knowledge of the English language and her deep understanding of the spirituality of St. Thérèse of Lisieux. I also wish to thank Fr. Edmund Lane, S.S.P. and the staff at Alba House for their continuous trust and support of my work.

Alexandra Plettenberg-Serban
New York
Feast of the Most Holy Trinity
June 6, 2004

Translator's Note

In order to assist the reader to get the most out of this book, I have

- added square brackets [ ] to indicate translations of titles that are not available in English,
- inserted [trans.] to explain historical or contemporary names, mentioned in the French text, that stem from a French theological or literary environment,
- indicated the English titles whenever the author mentioned a French title that is available in English, and included the page number for the quote.

For the Bible quotes, which are indicated in the text but not as footnotes, I have mostly used the New Revised Standard Version (N.R.S.V.) of the Holy Bible with the apocryphal and deuterocanonical books (American Bible Society: New York, 1989).

Introduction

In the Fall of 2001, after the very successful visit of the relics of St. Thérèse in Canada following the theme "Encountering Christ through St. Thérèse of Lisieux," I gave several retreats and conferences on her life and spirituality. During one of the televised sessions in Quebec, at the Mary Gatineau Center, Lise Turbide asked me if I would lead Canadian pilgrims to Lisieux to follow "in the footsteps of St. Thérèse." I declined her offer for several reasons, but I also told her I would nevertheless pray to St. Thérèse about her wish. It was a polite way to avoid the responsibility, fully realizing that you don't pray to St. Thérèse without her responding.

In November 2002, I went to Lisieux at the request of the religious Community of the Beatitudes to give a session entitled "St. Thérèse — A Hope for Couples and Families."[1] This experience turned out to be very inspiring especially since my wife was with me. When we returned to Paris, we went to the Basilica of the Sacred Heart in Montmartre for a time of quiet prayer. A Benedictine nun came up to me and I felt confronted point blank when she put before me the same issue that Ms. Turbide had in Canada: "Wouldn't you like to bring some pilgrims here for St. Thérèse?" I said to myself: Here is another person asking me; does this mean I should bring some Canadian pilgrims to Montmartre

---

[1] Jacques Gauthier, *Thérèse de Lisieux, une espérance pour les familles* [*Thérèse of Lisieux, a Hope for Families*. Not translated.], Nouan-le-Fuzelier, Éd. des Béatitudes, 2003, 144 pgs.

and Lisieux? I responded to her with the same words that are so easy to say: "Sister, pray. If St. Thérèse wishes it, it will happen." However as soon as I answered her, I already felt compelled to accept, which I did right away. St. Thérèse certainly didn't waste any time.

The Thirst of Jesus

In the midst of preparing the first pilgrimage, which was to end on November 2, 2003 with a session entitled "St. Thérèse and the Communion of Saints," news came that Mother Teresa would be beatified in Rome on Mission Sunday, October 19, 2003, the same day, six years earlier, that St. Thérèse of Lisieux had been proclaimed a Doctor of the Church. The message became clear and I immediately made plans to include in the pilgrimage a trip to Rome for the beatification of Mother Teresa who owed her name to St. Thérèse. We would be coming through Paris mainly to see the Basilica of the Sacred Heart and the Church of Our Lady of Victory, churches which were very important in the life of St. Thérèse, and would end the pilgrimage by praying and visiting the important sights in Lisieux and the surrounding area.

It was during this period that I felt deeply inspired to write a book about the two Theresas. I had already written several books about St. Thérèse, which led me to assume there was nothing left to say. The more I tried to dismiss this idea, the stronger it came back to me. I tried with every means I had to resist, but the first spark was there and that is what matters when I am about to undertake a new book. I spoke with my friend Christophe Rémond, Director of the publishing house Parole et Silence [Word and Silence], and he immediately supported the idea of this future book.

The question became: From which perspective should I approach the two Theresas? What was the deepest connection uniting the two? My search guided me more and more feverishly toward the "thirst of Jesus," not their thirst for Jesus but the thirst of Jesus for them, for us. What seemed to be profound to me was the common theme running through the spirituality of both St. Thérèse and Blessed Mother Teresa, namely,

- their need to console Jesus because of so many people's indifference to Him, and to quench His thirst for love;
- their need to please Him;
- their need to be open to the overflow of tenderness in His heart because His love is not received as it ought to be.

On February 6, 2003, I found this vibrant red thread, this common theme: the "thirst of Jesus." I asked for a sign from St. Thérèse — not out of a lack of faith, but out of excessive confidence. I developed the habit before going to bed of reading a quote of St. Thérèse from a little book which contains a collection of 365 of her sayings.[2] That night, as I opened the book, I asked her to guide me to one of her sayings that would invoke the theme of thirst and confirm in this way the theme of my proposed book. The text for February 6 was taken from Letter 196 to her oldest sister and godmother, Sister Marie of the Sacred Heart, a text which Mother Teresa often used to explain her mission to her sisters:

> …this same God, who declares He had no need to tell us if He is hungry, did not hesitate to *beg* for a little water from the Samaritan Woman. He was thirsty.… But when He said, "Give me to drink," it was the *love* of His poor creatures that the Creator of the universe was asking for. He was thirsty for love.… Ah! I feel it more than ever before, Jesus is *parched*, for He meets only the ungrateful and indifferent among His disciples in the world, and among *His own disciples*, alas, He finds

---

2 Raymond Zambelli, *Avec Thérèse de Lisieux, Rien que pour aujourd'hui* [*With Thérèse of Lisieux, Something Only for Today*. Not translated.], Strasbourg, Éditions du Signe, 2000.

few hearts who surrender to Him without reservations, who understand the real tenderness of His infinite Love.[3]

Don't think that I always receive answers that quickly and that clearly. There is nothing magic about it. Faith is a question of love and confidence in God especially in moments of spiritual dryness, as St. Thérèse has shown to me so often. My research into the writings of St. Thérèse and Blessed Mother Teresa have assured me that I didn't go wrong in making the connection between these two great lovers of God at the foot of the Cross. The cry of Jesus, "I thirst," has profoundly marked both of the women's writings, and determined their entire lives. Where those words are written next to each Crucifix in the houses of the Missionaries of Charity, a photo of St. Thérèse is usually not far away. Mother Teresa writes in her *Spiritual Testament* (which can be found in its entirety in Appendix 2):

> For me it is very clear that everything about the Missionaries of Charity (M.C.) is intended to quench the Thirst of Jesus. His words, written on the walls of all the chapels of the M.C.'s, are not of the past but living, here and now spoken to you. Do you believe them? If yes, you would hear and feel His presence.... If you would retain one thing from this letter, it should be this: "I thirst" is a much deeper phrase than if Jesus would have just said, "I love you." As long as you do not know in a very intimate way that Jesus is thirsty for you, it will be impossible for you to know who He wants to be for you, nor who He wants you to be for Him.

---

[3] *Letters of Saint Thérèse of Lisieux*, vol. II, translated by John Clarke, O.C.D., ICS Publications, Washington, DC, 1988, p. 995.

That thirst is also expressed in the encounter between Jesus and the Samaritan woman, the subject of Chapter 3: "Give me to drink" (Jn 4:7). We will hear the echo of these words resounding in the hearts of the two Theresas, and even within the third one, St. Teresa of Avila. In Chapter 4 of this book, I will come to another quote of Jesus which is also often cited in the writings of the two Theresas: "Amen, I say to you, whatever you did to one of the least brothers of mine, you did to me" (Mt 25:40). In the last chapter, we will return to the Cross, perceived as the wound of love of Jesus, magnificently expressed in a poem by St. John of the Cross about a shepherd forgotten by his shepherdess entitled: "A Lone Young Shepherd."

The Well Longs to Be Consumed

Both St. Thérèse and Blessed Mother Teresa often said that God is thirsty, to the displeasure of people who see God as an impersonal energy, and an unapproachable being of icy cold perfection. "The well longs to be consumed," said St. Gregory of Nyssa.[4] The revelation of this divine thirst leads to the core of the vocations of our two Theresas: namely, to be love in the Church and in the world. This vocation to love has never been so urgent as it is today. "Love is not loved," exclaimed St. Francis of Assisi in his time. Father Joseph Langford, Co-Founder with Mother Teresa of the branch of Priests of the Missionaries of Charity, points in the same direction when he writes: "We exist to quench the thirst that Christ has for our love and in a certain way God

---

[4] St. Gregory of Nyssa, 331/40-395, belongs to the Cappadocian Church Fathers from Asia Minor. Born of a deeply religious family, he became Bishop of Athens. He is noted for having written hundreds of homilies, among others some about the Song of Solomon and the Beatitudes. The author of several important theological works regarding the teachings of the Catholic Church and against Arianism, he also wrote about the Christian Life and how to live it [trans.].

'exists' in our lives to quench our existential thirst for His Love."[5]

God is known to us as an unknown, St. Thomas Aquinas said. He is always beyond what we could say about Him. But in His Son, he risked the revelation of who He is. His Word becoming flesh has given humanity a new chance, and has modeled a way of compassion that leads to this thirst for love and to be loved which Christ Himself has experienced to a degree which we will never be able to feel. In the appearance of the Son, the Father is revealed: "Whoever has seen me has seen the Father" (Jn 14:9).

"No one has ever seen God. It is God the only Son, who is close to the Father's heart, who has made Him known" (Jn 1:18). Christ reveals to us that God is thirsting for our thirst, that He desires to love us. Present in our soul, He wants to live in us completely with His merciful love. He also needs to give Himself to us in order to expand; that is His joy. I hear the two Theresas who seem to tell us: Let us not take from God the joy of loving us!

God Is Goodness Giving Himself Freely

Father Marie-Eugène of the Child Jesus, an important disciple of St. Thérèse, defines this tender God in the spirit of Pseudo-Dionysius[6] and St. Thomas Aquinas: "God is the *Bonum diffusivum sui*, which means Goodness, the Good that gives of

---

[5] Joseph Langford, "D'une Thérèse à l'autre" ["From one Thérèse to the Other." Not translated], *Feu et Lumière*, September 1997, p. 43. *Feu et Lumière* [*Fire and Light*] is a magazine published by the Community of the Beatitudes.

[6] Dionysius the Areopagite was a disciple of St. Paul mentioned in Acts 17:34. An unknown author of the late fifth or early sixth centuries appropriated his name and is known as Pseudo-Dionysius; his writings are about mystical theology and Christian philosophy. Greatly influenced by him were: Hildegard of Bingen (1098-1179), St. Thomas Aquinas (1125-1274), St. Catherine of Siena (1347-1380), St. Teresa of Avila (1515-1582), St. John of the Cross (1515-1582), and many more [trans.].

itself freely."[7] Love is its natural consequence. This giving action of divine mercy sustains us if we live in a filial relationship with God, when we allow Him to show us that we are indeed His beloved children. In this way we become His joy and fulfill His need to give Himself, because the God of love wants to communicate, to give, and pour Himself out; this is His nature: "The love of God has been poured into our hearts through the Holy Spirit which has been given to us" (Rm 5:5).

> If the Good would for a moment stop pouring itself out in loving act of self giving, it would no longer be love. Love that is arrested becomes egoism. God begets His Son infinitely, and from the Father and the Son the Holy Spirit proceeds constantly. This is because God is eternal love. Love that has been given to us should not stay in our souls. It needs to reconnect with its source and it wants to continue through us its drive to give of itself.[8]

St. Thérèse offers herself to merciful love in order to receive all the overflow of tenderness which is stored up in the heart of Christ. Blessed Mother Teresa quenches the thirst of Jesus in loving the poorest of the poor. These souls, which are filled with great desire, extend themselves in the measure of God's thirst for them. They understood that God suffers from not being able to give more of Himself; such is His justice overflowing with mercy.

---

[7] Louis Menvielle, *Thérèse Docteur racontée par le Père Marie-Eugène de l'Enfant-Jesus*, tome II. *Les clés de la Petite Voie* [*Thérèse as Doctor, explained by Father Marie-Eugène of the Child Jesus*, vol. II, *The keys to the Little Way*. Not translated]. Venasque et Saint Maur, Éd. Du Carmel et Éd. Parole et Silence, 1998, p. 37.

[8] Father Marie-Eugène, O.C.D., *I Want to See God*, vol. 1, The Fides Publishers Association, 1953, p. 361. Christian Classics published a one-volume edition of this work in 1997 in both hard and soft cover.

The Human God

Some call it anthropomorphism when you attribute human forms, reactions, and sentiments to the Most High. So what? Is this not what the authors of the Bible did and all the mystics who came after them? If God made His own image visible in the face of a human being, we can use analogies, symbols and comparisons in order to better understand what He is like. It is not so much God who acts like us, but we who should act like Him. In this respect, I prefer to speak about "theomorphism." When we desire God it is only because He desires us first. When we search for Him, it is because He searches for us first. When we believe and hope in Him, it is because He believes and hopes in us first. As Charles Péguy expressed so well:

> All the feelings that we might have for God, God had them first for us.... And everything we could have for God, God first had it for us.[9]

We can only speak about God in analogies, knowing that no concept is able to capture His mystery. In this sense, silence and poetry are the most appropriate language to approach this mystery. The poet of liturgy, Patrick de la Tour du Pin, speaks about "theopoetry" in the hope that many will become more aware of the mystery of God by singing about it, as did the mystics of Carmel. Father Éliane, a Carmelite musician and a well-known collector of poetic texts and songs from the mystics states: "I find it formidable that songs can become pathways to sainthood! God loves the 'little means' [poetry, singing, acting] as St. Thérèse of Lisieux said, beginning with the Incarnation. The greatest mysticism manifests the greatest humility and the greatest human ten-

---

[9] Charles Péguy, *Le Porche du mystère de la deuxième vertu* [*The Mystery of the Second Virtue*. Not translated.].

derness, contemplation of the Crib at the Cross."[10]

"God is love," St. John affirms. He allows the person to be free; free to receive Him or reject Him, free to enjoy Him or to hurt Him. He keeps us as children eternally for the life to come, but that does not happen without causing Him pain. God's mercy and compassion are all-powerful. Everything in Him is acceptance and gift, which is the very work of life and love. St. John of the Cross asks in the foreword of *The Spiritual Canticle*: Who can express what the Spirit allows those loving souls to hear in whom He resides?

> Who can describe in writing the understanding he gives to loving souls in whom he dwells? And who can express with words the experience he imparts to them? Who, finally, can explain the desires he gives them? Certainly, no one can! Not even they who receive these communications. As a result these persons let something of their experience overflow in figures, comparisons and similitudes, and from the abundance of their spirit pour out secrets and mysteries rather than rational explanations. If these similitudes are not read with the simplicity of the spirit of knowledge and love they contain, they will seem to be absurdities rather than reasonable utterances....[11]

Following the Good News of Salvation in Jesus Christ, we can express God through our limited words and respond to His thirst through our imperfect works. Nothing human is hidden from God. The wish to become divine has to begin by being fully

---

[10] Pierre Éliane, *Chansons du Carmel* [*Songs of Carmel*. Not translated.], Paris, Presses de la Renaissance, 2002, p. 20.

[11] *The Collected Works of Saint John of the Cross*, Translated by Kieran Kavanaugh, O.C.D., Otilio Rodriguez, O.C.D., Institute of Carmelite Studies, Washington, DC, 1991, Prologue, *The Spiritual Canticle*, p. 469.

human. Only our profound humanness reflects the unique light of the very nature of God, His thirst to love and to be loved. This humanness is embodied in such geniuses of love like St. Thérèse and Blessed Mother Teresa. They have consoled Jesus for the lack of love that He encounters through indifference, by opening themselves fully to receive the overflow of love from His heart. Their loving desire was to please Him by offering themselves without reservation, making love the only motive of their actions. "To please Jesus," was an expression very dear to the Little Flower, which became "Only all for Jesus" for Mother Teresa.

> St. Thérèse and Mother Teresa: two sisters in spirit, who are like two mirrors who mutually reflect each other, one revealing what at first glance is not obvious in the other.... St. Thérèse and Mother Teresa are the two witnesses whom God chose to reveal his Thirst for love, the vocation for all humanity to love and be loved, and the 'Little Way' open to all.[12]

---

[12] Joseph Langford, "D'une Thérèse à l'autre...", pp. 44-45.

I THIRST

Biblical Abbreviations

OLD TESTAMENT

Genesis	Gn	Nehemiah	Ne	Baruch	Ba
Exodus	Ex	Tobit	Tb	Ezekiel	Ezk
Leviticus	Lv	Judith	Jdt	Daniel	Dn
Numbers	Nb	Esther	Est	Hosea	Ho
Deuteronomy	Dt	1 Maccabees	1 M	Joel	Jl
Joshua	Jos	2 Maccabees	2 M	Amos	Am
Judges	Jg	Job	Jb	Obadiah	Ob
Ruth	Rt	Psalms	Ps	Jonah	Jon
1 Samuel	1 S	Proverbs	Pr	Micah	Mi
2 Samuel	2 S	Ecclesiastes	Ec	Nahum	Na
1 Kings	1 K	Song of Songs	Sg	Habakkuk	Hab
2 Kings	2 K	Wisdom	Ws	Zephaniah	Zp
1 Chronicles	1 Ch	Sirach	Si	Haggai	Hg
2 Chronicles	2 Ch	Isaiah	Is	Malachi	Ml
Ezra	Ezr	Jeremiah	Jr	Zechariah	Zc
		Lamentations	Lm		

NEW TESTAMENT

Matthew	Mt	Ephesians	Eph	Hebrews	Heb
Mark	Mk	Philippians	Ph	James	Jm
Luke	Lk	Colossians	Col	1 Peter	1 P
John	Jn	1 Thessalonians	1 Th	2 Peter	2 P
Acts	Ac	2 Thessalonians	2 Th	1 John	1 Jn
Romans	Rm	1 Timothy	1 Tm	2 John	2 Jn
1 Corinthians	1 Cor	2 Timothy	2 Tm	3 John	3 Jn
2 Corinthians	2 Cor	Titus	Tt	Jude	Jude
Galatians	Gal	Philemon	Phm	Revelation	Rv

CHAPTER ONE

Saint Thérèse of Lisieux: To Console Jesus

The whole life of Thérèse Martin was a burning desire, a consuming love. Here is her secret: "To *love* Jesus with *passion*" (MsA 47v).[1] His name, His face, His presence ravished her heart: "Christ is my Love, He is my whole life" (PN 26).[2] To please Him is her one and only joy: "My only joy on earth is to be able to please You" (PN 45).[3] She consoled Him in the most insignificant gestures: "...in order to console Jesus He wants only a *look*, a *sigh*, but a look and a sigh that are for *Him alone!*" (LT 96)[4]

We see it; St. Thérèse is first and foremost an immensely loving person. Six months before her death she writes: "...for I shall desire in heaven the same thing as I do on earth: To love Jesus and to make Him loved" (LT 220).[5] She now spends her

---

[1] MsA 47 v means manuscript (Ms) A, back or reverse (verso) side of page 47 in the original manuscript, whereas r (recto) means the front of the original page. For our quotation and pagination, we will be using *Story of a Soul*, Third Edition, translated by John Clarke, O.C.D., ICS Publications, Washington, DC, 1996, in which this quote will be found on page 102 [trans.].

[2] *The Poetry of Saint Thérèse of Lisieux*, translated by Donald Kinney, O.C.D., ICS Publications, Washington, DC, 1996, p. 137.

[3] *Ibid.*, p. 186.

[4] *Letters of Saint Thérèse of Lisieux*, vol. I, translated by John Clarke, O.C.D., ICS Publications, Washington, DC, 1982, p. 588.

[5] *Letters of Saint Thérèse of Lisieux*, vol. II, translated by John Clarke, O.C.D., ICS Publications, Washington, DC, 1988, p. 1060.

heaven doing good on earth, showering earth with roses, as she expressed it herself. Which reminds us of the unfathomable, and never before known success of her relics traveling the world.

In the Fall of 2001, I had the grace to travel with the relics of St. Thérèse for one month to Quebec, Canada. The churches everywhere were filled around the clock to the astonishment of the clergy and religious. It was very moving to see people of all ages and in all physical and emotional conditions, pray before the mortal remains of the Saint. It is difficult to explain such a phenomenon because this young woman had seemingly done nothing extraordinary, if we use an old exclusive understanding of holiness, which included visions, stigmata, healings, etc. St. Thérèse was called to holiness by understanding and living a call to love in the ordinary world of daily life. People seem to relate to her proclaimed "littleness." The "phenomenon of St. Thérèse" belongs to the mystery of God, as St. Paul expressed it: "God chose what is foolish in the world to shame the wise; God chose what is weak in the world to shame the strong" (1 Cor 1:27).

To Live of Love

Two words express St. Thérèse in her entirety: "To live of love."[6] Her spiritual itinerary, which is simple and profound at the same time, was nothing less than a long act of love. After Thérèse Martin was born in Alençon, France on January 2, 1873, she had to be placed in the care of a wet nurse in Semaillé, a small village approximately six miles from her home, since she was already sick with a digestive illness. A peasant named Rose Taillé [a name

---

6   For biographical and spiritual studies of Thérèse of Lisieux please read my books: *Toi, l'amour, Thérèse de Lisieux*; and *Thérèse de l'Enfant Jesus, docteur de L'Église* [*You are Love, Thérèse of Lisieux*; and *Thérèse of the Child Jesus and the Holy Face, Doctor of the Church*. None of them has been translated into English.], éditions Anne Sigier.

which means "cut fresh rose," trans.] nursed her for one year in her farmhouse. From the age of four on, she was determined to "choose all" which was her response when her sister offered her a basket full of toys, and instead of choosing one toy she wanted to take all of them. This became a determining factor in the development of her spirituality in her later life. Her mother died of cancer in the same year. Two of her older sisters entered the Carmel of Lisieux and St. Thérèse felt abandoned. The separations made her psychologically very fragile and when she fell gravely ill, the smile of the Virgin Mary healed her in 1883. On Christmas Eve in 1886, after returning from Midnight Mass, she experienced her "conversion" as she called it, a victory over her self-love, which opened her to a new intimacy with Jesus.

> On that *night* of *light* the third period of my life began, the most beautiful of all, the one in which I received the *most graces* from heaven.... The work I had been unable to do in ten years was done by Jesus in one instant and He even was content just with my *good will*, which I always had plenty of. Like His apostles I could say to Him: "Master, I fished all night but caught nothing" (Lk 5:5). Even more merciful to me than He was to His disciples, He *took* the net *Himself*, cast it and drew it in filled with fish.... He made me a fisher of *souls*, I experienced a great desire to work for the conversion of sinners, a desire I hadn't felt so intensely before....
> I felt *charity* enter into my soul, and the need to forget myself and to please others; since then I've been happy! (MsA 45v).[7]

---

7   *Story of a Soul*, translated by John Clarke, O.C.D., ICS Publications, Washington, DC, 1996, pp. 98-99.

To Quench the Thirst of Jesus

The grace of freedom from self-love meant for St. Thérèse that she was given the experience of salvation which Christ has offered to all of us, especially to the poorest of the poor. Progress was made in the healing of the profound wounds of her childhood. Thérèsian specialists have so emphasized the importance of this event that another equally important revelation which had immense repercussions in her life can easily be overshadowed; her discovery of the thirst of Jesus. She tells us about this major event which took place immediately after her Christmas conversion:

> One Sunday, looking at a picture of Our Lord on the Cross I was struck by the blood flowing from one of the divine hands. I felt a great pang of sorrow when thinking this blood was falling on the ground in my prayer-book, the blood that was flowing from one of His Divine hands shocked me. I experienced a great pain when I was thinking of the blood dripping on the floor and nobody would rush to collect it and I decided to stay at the foot of the cross in order to receive the Divine dew which continued to flow. I understood that I needed to distribute it to souls.... Jesus' cry on the Cross resounded continually in my heart: 'I thirst!' These words ignited in me an unknown and very living fire.... I wanted to give my Beloved to drink and I felt myself consumed with a *thirst* for *souls*. As yet, it was not the souls of priests that attracted me, but those of *great sinners*; I *burned* with the desire to snatch them from the eternal flames (MsA 45v).[8]

---

8   *Ibid.*, p. 99.

4

Pranzini

St. Thérèse's zeal for Jesus grew outside of her immediate environment. Her passionate love for Him inspired her to find the means to console Jesus who thirsts for souls. She found a way by praying for sinners. The sign she received concerning Pranzini, a man condemned to death for having strangled two women and one girl, and for whom she had ardently prayed, confirmed that she has chosen the right way. She told us about the transformation that happened in her:

> To awaken my zeal God showed me my desires were pleasing to Him. I heard talk of a great criminal just condemned to death for some horrible crimes;[9] everything pointed to the fact that he would die impenitent. I wanted at all costs to prevent him from falling into hell, and to attain my purpose I employed every means imaginable. Feeling that of myself I could do nothing, I offered to God all the infinite merits of Our Lord, the treasures of the Church, and finally I begged Céline to have a Mass offered for my intentions. I didn't dare ask this myself for fear of being obliged to say it was for Pranzini, the great criminal. I didn't even want to tell Céline, but she asked me such tender and pressing questions, I confided my secret to her. Far from laughing at me, she asked if she could help convert *my sinner*. I accepted gratefully, for I would have wished all creatures would unite with me to beg grace for the guilty man.
>
> I felt in the depth of my heart *certain* that our desires would be granted, but to obtain courage to pray

---

9   At the age of 31, Henri Pranzini, in the course of an attempted jewelry robbery, strangled two women and a twelve-year-old child in Paris on March 17, 1887. On August 31, 1887 he was put to death by the guillotine. Thérèse called him "My first child" [trans.].

for sinners I told God I was sure He would pardon the poor unfortunate Pranzini; that I'd believe this even if he went to his death without *any sign of repentance* or without *having gone to confession.* I was absolutely confident in the mercy of Jesus. But I was begging Him for a "*sign*" of repentance just for my own simple consolation.

My prayer was answered to the letter! In spite of Papa's prohibition that we read no papers, I didn't think I was disobeying when reading the passages pertaining to Pranzini. The day after his execution I found the newspaper "*La Croix.*" I opened it quickly and what did I see? Ah! my tears betrayed my emotion and I was obliged to hide. Pranzini had not gone to confession. He had mounted the scaffold and was preparing to place his head in the formidable opening, when suddenly, seized by an inspiration, he turned, took hold of the *crucifix* the priest was holding out to him and *kissed* the *sacred wounds three times!* Then his soul went to receive the *merciful* sentence of Him who declares that in heaven "there will be more joy over one sinner who does penance than over ninety-nine just who have no need of repentance!" (Lk 15:7).

I had obtained the "sign" I requested and this sign was a perfect replica of the grace Jesus had given me when He attracted me to pray for sinners. Wasn't it before the *wounds of Jesus* when seeing His Divine *blood* flowing that the thirst for souls had entered my heart? I wished to give them this *immaculate blood* to drink, this blood which was to purify them from their stains, and the lips of my "*first child*" were pressed to the sacred wounds!

What an unspeakable sweet response! After this unique grace my desire to save souls grows each day, and I seemed to hear Jesus say to me what He said to the Samaritan woman: *"Give me to drink!"* (Jn 4:7). It was a true interchange of love: to souls I was giving the *blood of Jesus,* to Jesus I was offering these same souls refreshed by the *divine dew.* I slaked His thirst and the more I gave Him *to drink,* the more the thirst of my poor little soul increased, and it was this ardent thirst He was giving me as the most delightful drink of His love (MsA 45v-46v).[10]

The Cry of Jesus on the Cross

St. Thérèse understood that the cry of Jesus on the Cross was much more than just that of a dying man's agony, even if it reminds us of people in their last struggle who are completely dehydrated and dying of thirst. She wrote: "I have received the grace to understand more than ever how much Jesus desires to be loved" (MsA 84r).[11] Also that "…He does not need our works, but only our *love…*" (MsB 1v).[12] With His cry, Jesus fulfills the Scriptures and identifies with the thirst for love of the suffering servant, the suffering of mankind.

> I am utterly exhausted from crying out;
> my throat burns.
> When I was thirsty, they gave me vinegar.
> (Ps 69:4, 22)

St. Thérèse welcomed the cry, "I thirst" (Jn 19:28), and united herself with Christ in His deprivation on the Cross. She spent the rest of her life responding to the cry of Jesus by mothering and caressing Him in others. She wanted to console Jesus who

---

10 *Story of a Soul,* pp. 99-101.
11 *Ibid.,* p. 180.
12 *Ibid.,* p. 189.

died deprived of everything after He was made thirsty. "After He took the vinegar, Jesus said: 'It is finished.' Then He bowed His head and gave up His spirit" (Jn 19:30) and it was Pranzini who would quench the thirst of Jesus like the Good Thief next to Jesus on the Cross. With Pranzini, St. Thérèse began her active and spiritual apostolate and became Patroness of the Missions.

Jesus loved until the end when He died, as He had wished: "Jesus, having loved His people who were in the world, loved them to the very end" (Jn 13:1). His filial obedience to His Father became His true thirst, as it did for St. Thérèse: "Will I refuse the cup that my Father gave me to drink?" (Jn 18:11). On December 26, 1896, St. Thérèse wrote to Father Maurice Bellière, one of the two missionary priests with whom her Prioress had assigned her to correspond: "It is very consoling to think that Jesus, the Strong God, knew our weaknesses, that He trembled at the sight of the bitter chalice, this chalice that He had in the past so ardently desired to drink" (LT 213).[13]

The mission of Jesus to announce the Good News of the Kingdom and to reveal the love of the Father became His great hunger: "My food is to do the will of Him who sent Me and to bring His work to completion" (Jn 4:34). He dies giving back His life to the Father and returning to Him. Jesus spoke so well of the Father that the Father corroborated His mission by raising Him from the dead. "God raised this Jesus — and of this we are all witnesses. When He was, therefore, exalted at the right hand of God and had received from the Father the promise of the Holy Spirit, He has poured it forth, as you can both see and hear" (Ac 2:32, 33). The Church, born from the open heart of Jesus and from the Holy Spirit, will no longer be alone: "And I will be with you always until the end of time" (Mt 28:20). In fact the Resurrected Christ will always be our Emmanuel, which means God with us, who will incessantly pour Himself forth, to give of Himself.

---

[13] *Letters of Saint Thérèse of Lisieux*, vol. II, p. 1042.

The Little Way

St. Thérèse was a woman with the desire to quench the thirst of Jesus. Her visit with Pope Leo XIII showed her unusual determination. At the age of fifteen she entered the Carmel of Lisieux because of Jesus and not for her sisters. Religious life did not present any illusions for her. Her ascent to Carmel was spectacular and her progress was steady, thanks to her "Little Way" of holiness, which she discovered in the texts of the Bible. To respond to the "I thirst" of Jesus is the way *par excellence*, wherein the poor in spirit quench His thirst and let themselves be loved by Him.

On that little way our limitations are not an obstacle, but the very means to take the "elevator of love" which St. Thérèse experienced as the arms of Jesus lifting us up to His heart. She compared our weaknesses and failures to children, who were not quite able to walk safely on their own, and needed to be picked up after their occasional falls. Understanding the fear of so many people, St. Thérèse proposed the opposite: confidence. Her God was nothing but mercy, far from a God of vengeance: "My way is all confidence and love, I do not understand souls who fear a friend so tender" (LT 226).[14]

Even if she frequently fell asleep at prayer time, confidence had the last word: "I should be desolate for having slept (for seven years) during my hours of prayer and my *thanksgiving* after Holy Communion; still, I am not desolate.... I remember that the *little children* are as pleasing to their parents when they are asleep as well as when they are wide awake" (MsA 75v).[15] What matters is the intention of the heart. What was important for St. Thérèse was to be open to receiving Jesus, this beggar of love, who asks us, as He did the Samaritan woman: "Give me to drink." St. Thérèse moved ever deeper towards this central motif of the Little

---

[14]   *Letters*, vol. II, p. 1093.

[15]   *Story of a Soul*, p. 165.

Way: Jesus' thirst for our love, which can be quenched by those of us who are poor in spirit. They are privileged members of the Kingdom who are close to the Beatitudes, like those of us who are unable to see and yet through the grace of conversion, receive the ability to see like Zechariah, the Samaritan woman, Mary Magdalene, the Good Thief. She also offers herself to merciful love to receive the overflow of tenderness, which is stored up in Jesus' heart, because there are too few souls who allow God to love them as only He can love.

On June 11, 1895, kneeling with Céline before the statue of the Virgin of the Smile, St. Thérèse proclaimed her Act of Oblation to Merciful Love, which is reproduced in this book as Appendix One. This text testifies to her immense desire: to be open to divine mercy and quench His thirst to love us, which should burn in every faithful person. Several months before she wrote about Love being misunderstood, in a short play entitled *Les Anges à la crèche* [*The Angels at the Manger*], she wrote: "O Jesus! Why must it be that so much love is not understood?"[16] It is this troublesome feeling of ignored love, which brought forth her prayer of Oblation to Merciful Love. In her third play entitled *Joan of Arc Accomplishes her Mission* she speaks in the voice of Jesus:

> I have made them — the souls — for Myself,
> I made their desires infinite,
> The least soul who loves Me,
> Becomes Paradise for Me. (Play 3)

God does not impose Himself, He offers Himself freely; we do not own Him, He gives Himself freely. "The one who comes

---

[16] *Saint Thérèse de L'Enfant-Jesus et de la Sainte-Face*, NEC, Edition du Cerf, 1992 Desclée de Brouwer, *Récréations Pieuses, Prières*, pp. 7-474. [Thérèse of Lisieux wrote 8 plays which are not yet translated. Our quotes are from play No. 2: *The Angels at the Manger of Jesus* (1894), and No. 3: *Joan of Arc Accomplishes Her Mission* (1895). Quotes translated by the translator.]

and begs from you / He is the Eternal Word" (Play 5).[17] St. Thérèse offered herself to Him with empty hands and an open heart. This Act of Oblation marks a significant change in the history of Christian spirituality. St. Thérèse carried the text on her heart together with the Gospels.

The Thérèsian Way, which is called "The Way of Spiritual Childhood," has strongly inspired Blessed Mother Teresa, as we will see in the following chapter, and is not reserved for the elite. It is a way that we can apply from the beginning of our spiritual life onward "with the absolute certainty that God's Mercy will extend to all souls who offer themselves to Him."[18] This new way, straight and direct, brings us progressively towards the summit of abandonment and love, culminating in the desire of Jesus to love and to be loved. The way ascends gently in the measure of our confidence; the more faithful we proceed with it, the more we learn about abandonment, the more we become able to give ourselves over to this "science of love," the more we become able to be open to divine mercy which will penetrate everything.

Discovering this little way means to encounter Christ. The way is already traced out for us by St. Thérèse, who pointed to its spiritual attitudes: "*Surrender* of the little child, which falls asleep without fear in the arms of its father" (MsB 1r).[19] Prayer flows from this spirit of a child and from confidence. St. Thérèse gave us her beautiful definition: "For me *prayer* is an aspiration of the heart, it is a simple glance directed to heaven, it is a cry of gratitude and love in the midst of trial as well as joy; finally it is something great, supernatural, which expands my soul and unites me to Jesus" (MsC 25r-25v).[20]

St. Thérèse's life and spirituality is a way that leads us to Jesus.

---

[17] No. 5: *The Divine Little Beggar of Christmas.*

[18] Louis Menvielle, *Thérèse Docteur racontée par le Père Marie-Eugène* [*Thérèse as Doctor, explained by Father Marie-Eugène of the Child Jesus.* Not translated.], Vol. II, p. 273.

[19] *Story of a Soul*, p. 188.

[20] *Ibid.*, p. 242.

Her truth brings us to the Gospel of Jesus, her life gives witness to the resurrection of Jesus. She opposed doubt and uncertainty, and strongly encouraged a total confidence in Jesus. Her path is not burdensome, but it is light because she joyfully accepted her limitations. In this world where we are such victims of fear and suspicion, she never stops urging us to entrust everything to confidence in oneself, in others, and in God. She wrote to Father Bellière:

> Regarding those who *love* Him and who come after each indelicacy to ask His pardon by throwing themselves into His arms, Jesus is thrilled with joy. He says to His angels what the father of the prodigal son said to his servants: 'Clothe him in his best robe, and place a ring on his finger, and let us rejoice.' Ah! how little known are the *goodness*, the *merciful love* of Jesus, Brother!… It is true, to enjoy these treasures one must humble oneself, recognize one's nothingness, and that is what many souls do not want to do; but, little Brother, this is not the way you act, so the way of simple and loving confidence is really made for you (LT 261).[21]

The Science of Love

The only science to which St. Thérèse aspires is the science of the saints, what she calls "the science of love," of which confidence is the central element: "Oh! how I would like to be able to make you understand what I feel!… It is confidence and nothing but confidence that must lead us to love…. Since we see the *way*, let us run together" (LT 197).[22]

---

[21] *Letters*, vol. II, p. 1164.
[22] *Ibid.*, p. 1000.

St. Thérèse learned an important lesson from her deep understanding and experience of the thirst of Jesus; it is sufficient to be and to love. It is not necessary to impress or to prove that one of us is better than another. Of utmost importance is to love with all that we are, with all that we have, and to do so without feeling discouraged or defeated. She defines herself as being love in the heart of the Church: "My Vocation, at last I have found it, my VOCATION IS LOVE!... In the heart of the Church, my Mother, I shall be LOVE... thus I shall be everything... thus my dream will be realized" (MsB 3v).[23]

This is what I admire about her, her gift of self in the little things of daily life, this desire to love Jesus by only holding on to His Mercy. This joyful abandonment on her little way of confidence, her extraordinary hope to give herself for the salvation of others, was crystallized in her desire to be love in the heart of the Church, by receiving suffering like a grace and quenching the thirst of Jesus. Her strong desire and her extravagant dreams, to travel to the four corners of the world, is her passionate call to proclaim the Gospel and testify to Divine Mercy. Did this not deeply inspire Blessed Mother Teresa? She felt close to her, this sister and friend who is very active in the Communion of Saints: "I promise to have you taste after my departure for eternal life the happiness one can find in feeling a friendly soul next to oneself" (LT 261).[24]

On September 30, 1897, at the age of 24, St. Thérèse died of tuberculosis after great physical and spiritual suffering, experiencing a tormenting dark night of faith, which foreshadowed the religious skepticism of the twentieth century. Others, who would continue after her, like Marthe Robin[25] and Blessed Mother Ter-

---

[23] *Story of a Soul*, p. 194.

[24] *Letters*, vol. II, p. 1163.

[25] Marthe Robin (1902-1981) had mystical experiences and stigmata on Fridays from 1930-1932. She was the Foundress of the spiritual centers for retreats: *Homes of Charity*, recognized by the Pontifical Council for the Laity in 1986 [trans.]. See also her biography, *Marthe Robin*, by Rev. Raymond Peyret, New York, Alba House, 1983.

esa, would be tried with the same excruciating darkness. St. Thérèse wrote to Father Bellière on June 9, 1897: "I am not dying, I am entering into Life, and all that I cannot say to you here below, I will make you understand from the heights of heaven" (LT 244).[26]

Pope Pius XI canonized Thérèse of the Child Jesus and the Holy Face in 1925. She was proclaimed Patroness of the Missions in 1927,[27] and Secondary Patron of France with St. Joan of Arc in 1944. Finally, in 1997 she was declared the thirty-third Doctor of the Church by Pope John Paul II. Her book, *Story of a Soul,* which she wrote in obedience, has been continuously reissued and translated in more than 60 languages. "All is grace,"[28] she said one day — all Christianity can be summed up in this one word.

---

[26] *Letters,* vol. II, p. 1128.

[27] Msgr. Ovide Charlebois (1862-1933) was a Canadian Oblate of the Immaculate Mary. He became Apostolic Vicar in Keewatin, the far North of Canada. He sent a request to Rome, signed by more than 200 Missionary Bishops from all over the world asking that St. Thérèse may be declared Patron of the Missions, which took place in 1927 [trans.].

[28] *Last Conversations,* p. 57.

CHAPTER TWO

Blessed Mother Teresa:
To Quench the Thirst of Jesus

For Blessed Mother Teresa to love was to act. All her life she walked the Little Way of St. Thérèse of Lisieux by living her life with confidence and total abandonment to God the Father. She understood the main ideas of this little way of confident love, namely:

- to put oneself unconditionally and unalterably in the hands of God our Father, even if all seems lost.
- not to conceive of any other but Him alone for our strength and help.
- to refuse doubt and discouragement, to hand over all our anguish and sorrow to Our Lord and continue to advance in perfect freedom.
- to dare to be without fear of obstacles, knowing that nothing is impossible with God.
- to count on God our Father for everything with the spontaneous abandonment of little children, being totally convinced of our total need for Him, but at the same time being boldly reassured, if necessary, of His fatherly goodness.[1]

---

[1]   Mother Teresa, *No Greater Love…*, New World Library, Novato, California, 2002, p. 63.

The one who was called "mother" will respond to a particular call from Jesus who makes her the messenger of God's love for the poorest of the poor. Christ chose her for Himself to quench His thirst for souls. Mother Teresa knew it and repeated it often to her congregation: "Are we just another congregation? Why do we exist? We exist to quench the thirst of Jesus, to proclaim the love of Christ, and Jesus' thirst for souls."[2] That call was the key to her vocation; belonging to Jesus to whom she was passionately committed; from Him she derived her love for the world. "We are called to love the world. And God loved the world so much that He gave us Jesus. Today He loves the world so much that He gives you and me to be His Love, His compassion, and His presence through a life of prayer, of sacrifice and of surrender to God."[3]

Blessed Mother Teresa's Model: St. Thérèse

The energetic Blessed Mother Teresa had a good sense of humor; she often introduced herself in this fashion: "By blood I call myself Albanian, by citizenship Indian, by religion Catholic, by my mission I belong to the whole world, but my heart belongs only to Jesus."[4] Her love for Jesus always took precedence until she was finally called to let herself be fully clothed in Him in order to radiate His presence everywhere.

Agnes Gonxha Bojaxhiu was born on August 26, 1910 of Albanian parents in Skopje, Macedonia. She was baptized the next morning in the parish church of the Sacred Heart. Her father

---

2   Quoted in Joseph Langford, "D'une Thérèse à l'autre" ["From one Thérèse to the Other." Not translated.], p. 45. [See page xviii, note 5.]

3   Mother Teresa, *No Greater Love*, p. 12.

4   Quoted in Sister Monique-Marie of the Holy Face, "Thérèse de Lisieux, Teresa de Calcutta. Aimer selon le coeur de Dieu" ["Thérèse of Lisieux, Teresa of Calcutta. Love with the Heart of God." Not translated.], in: *Thérèse de Lisieux*, September, 1998, p. 32. This is a monthly magazine published by the central Office of Lisieux.

Nikola died when she was nine years old and her mother Drana had to take care of the family and raise her three children alone. Agnes went to the local public school and learned from her mother's example to help and share with the poor. Agnes was interested in the lives of the saints and stories about missionaries which she discovered and learned about as a member of the Legion of Mary. At the age of 12, almost coinciding with the beatification of St. Thérèse of Lisieux which had a great impact on the world and also on her own life, she experienced for the first time the call to religious life. The Croatian Jesuit, Father Franko Jambrenkovic was the pastor of the Catholic parish in Skopje and guided Agnes in prayer. When he received a new French edition of *Story of a Soul*, he started to translate passages for the children in the parish and he told Agnes about the canonization of St. Thérèse. She was totally overjoyed and felt confident that she could trust St. Thérèse completely to guide her along the way that God Himself had carved out for her.

Blessed Mother Teresa, who avoided talking about herself, kept secret the connection she had with St. Thérèse. In 1996, one year before she died, a journalist prying for new information achieved his goal, and Mother Teresa revealed her relationship to St. Thérèse:

> For us Christians, the canonization of a saint, like St. Thérèse of Lisieux, was a big event. For me, in any case, it seemed to be the greatest event in the first quarter of the century, much more significant than the First World War. I considered myself privileged to be alive at that moment. It was so strong, so beautiful, to live at such a time. I have never felt happier even when I took my final vows. I have rarely felt the kind of happiness that I knew then, when I understood that the "Little Flower" belonged forever in my life and that she would be an example for me. I can't remember the first

time I read her autobiography, or heard someone speak about her. Was it through my mother or that young Croatian priest? It is too long ago! It seems to me that she has always been there, close to me, as if she were truly a part of my family![5]

Religious Educator

The young Croatian Jesuit introduced Agnes to the Sisters of Our Lady of Loretto, also called the "Irish Ladies," who were very active in India. Agnes had asked the Lord for a sign and she was heard. Admitted as a postulant at the age of 18, she left for Dublin, learned English, and was sent to India to begin her novitiate. Agnes made her temporary vows on May 24, 1931. She changed her baptismal name to Teresa. She was very touched by the simplicity of St. Thérèse who showed her love for Jesus in the things of daily life. "To lead a Christian life allows our faith to grow. Many saints have gone before us to guide us, but I love those who are simple like St. Thérèse of Lisieux, the Little Flower of Jesus. I chose her as my namesake because she did ordinary things with extraordinary love."[6]

She refers to the love of St. Thérèse in another text: "When St. Thérèse, the 'Little Flower' was canonized, sometime after her death everybody asked themselves: 'Why did the Holy Father canonize her? She did nothing extraordinary.' The Holy Father's reason for his decision was given in writing: 'I want to canonize her because she has done ordinary things with extraordinary love.'"[7]

---

[5]   Quoted in: Perle Scemla, *Thérèse, Teresa. La Passion en Heritage* [*Thérèse, Teresa. Love as a legacy*. Not translated.], Paris, Éditions no 1, 1997, p. 12.

[6]   Quoted in: Jean Michel de Falco, *Mère Teresa, les miracles de la foi* [*Mother Teresa, Miracles of Faith*. Not translated.], Montreal, Québécor, 1997, p. 63.

[7]   Mother Teresa, *Nous serons jugés sur l'amour* [*We will be Judged on Love*. Not translated.], Paris, Mediaspaul, 1987, p. 152.

For seven years, Mother Teresa lived happily in Calcutta where she was a teacher at St. Mary's School, run by the Sisters of Our Lady of Loretto. She made her final vows in 1937. She taught history and geography, with a special focus for the young girls on the glorious past of their country, India. Later she became the Principal of a high school of Bengali children in central Calcutta. But her first vocation was going to be to love the poorest of the poor.

At the Service of the Poor

On September 10, 1946 as Blessed Mother Teresa prayed on the train en route to Darjeeling for her annual retreat, she felt deeply inspired by the Holy Spirit to give herself completely to the service of the poorest of the poor. She called this day the "Day of Inspiration," or "the call within the call." Jesus made her feel His immense thirst for love; He wanted to be consoled in His poor people who are the most precious to Him. "The message was quite clear. I was to leave the convent and consecrate myself completely to help the poor and live among them. It was an order. I knew where I belonged, but I did not know how to get there."[8]

Mother Teresa knew she was chosen like the great characters in the Bible: Abraham, Elijah, Isaiah, Jeremiah... and, above all, Jesus and St. Paul. This was the keystone of her mystique, of her passionate drive. The certainty of the call of Jesus became real in her identification with Him; she only wanted to belong to Him, she wanted to quench His thirst for souls and it is He whom she found in the suffering of the poor. There was not only St. Thérèse of Lisieux in Blessed Mother Teresa, but also St. Francis of Assisi who had the same commitment to the Gospels, the same asceticism, the same joy and the same freedom to choose and act.

---

[8] Mother Teresa, *No Greater Love...*, p. 195.

At the age of 38, Rome granted her permission to live a consecrated life outside her convent. She removed the habit of the Sisters of Loretto and donned the white sari with the blue trim and the cross on the shoulder, a symbol of her will to imitate Mary and to serve Christ in the poor. A young girl from her former school expressed her desire to consecrate herself to God as well and joined her. Others followed. In 1950 the Order of the Missionaries of Charity was officially born. As the source of the work of her new community, Mother Teresa focused on prayer for strength in trials and as an expression of joy: silent prayer, adoration before the Blessed Sacrament, the liturgy, and the Rosary. "Prayer enlarges the heart until it is capable of containing God's gift of Himself."[9]

In 1952, Blessed Mother Teresa opened a Hospice for the Dying, a symbol of her mission of compassion and joy towards the most deprived. She wanted the dying to experience human and divine love at least for the short time left to them. It was her thinking that she would give back to them their dignity as children of God. Her love did not expect anything in return. She was happy to serve and give a smile in the name of Jesus Christ, as her patroness St. Thérèse of Lisieux had done. Blessed Mother Teresa often said: "It is the intensity of love which we put into our gestures which makes them into something beautiful for God."[10]

"How do you do it, taking care of so many people?" somebody asked Blessed Mother Teresa. "I take care of one person and when I finish with that one person I commit myself to the next."[11] She took the time to hear and to love each person that she met as if that person were Christ. From there came the joy and the smile which she transmitted to us. Her sisters also reflected this joy and

---

[9] *Ibid.*, p. 4.

[10] *Ibid.*, p. 26.

[11] Thérèse Baudry, *Séjour chez Mère Teresa* [*Spending Time in the Presence of Mother Teresa.* Not translated.], Montréal, Meridien, 1988, pp. 157–158.

love which the world media found so appealing. Each member of the Missionaries of Charity becomes for others the face of Christ.

God's Hunger

Blessed Mother Teresa traveled the world to talk, to give witness, to visit her sisters, and to find the means to help the poor. She moved from one to the other to give each person what he or she needed, always saying the Rosary in the middle of the crowd. She urged us to love the poor who are in our families, and in our midst, because true poverty is a hunger for love, and a hunger for God.

"You in the West have the spiritually poorest of the poor much more than you have the physically poor. Often among the rich are people who are very spiritually poor."[12] This poverty comes from the absence of love. Blessed Mother Teresa often reminded us that in our families, we sometimes have someone who feels lonely, sick and in physical or emotional pain. We need to be there for the poorest among ourselves in giving them of our time until it really hurts. To love at the school of Mother Teresa is to give everything even if it causes us pain and inconvenience.

Jesus had experienced this hunger for love when He came among His own and they did not welcome Him. When He fed the crowds with five loaves of bread and two fish, it was the hunger for love which He wanted to satisfy. When He made the humble Blessed Mother Teresa with her Sisters His instruments, He equally wished to satisfy the hunger for love, which causes so much pain to all human beings.

Blessed Mother Teresa acted by founding more houses, meeting Christ in the desperation of the poor. Did she not add

---

12   Mother Teresa, *No Greater Love...*, p. 94.

to the three vows of poverty, chastity and obedience the fourth vow of charity towards the poor: *"A wholehearted and free service to the poorest of the poor"*? For herself and her sisters there was no doubt that it is Jesus in them who gathers the dying in Calcutta, relieves the lonely people in New York, helps the victims of earthquakes in Guatemala, crosses the lines of fire in Beirut and fights against abortion by adopting children. She wrote:

> I have taken it upon myself to represent the poor of the entire world: the unwanted, those who nobody wants, rejects, victims of abuse, the blind, the lepers, the alcoholics, those who are at the margins of society, all those who have come so far to have forgotten what human warmth and affection mean, and contact with others. (…) I would never touch a leper for all the money in the world offered to me, but I do it gratuitously out of the goodness of my heart filled with the love of God. (…) Those who nowadays ignore and push the poor away ignore and push Christ away. The poor honor us by allowing us to serve them.[13]

The Fruitfulness of Prayer

Blessed Mother Teresa was once asked what she does in the countries she travels to, and she responded spontaneously: "I come to see." She referred to the good old method of Catholic Action: see, judge, and act. In order to act one has to see. Unfortunately we look at things without seeing them. Blessed Mother Teresa said that in order to see things one had to pray. "Often a profound and fervent gaze at Christ makes up the best prayer: I look at Him

---

[13] Mother Teresa, *In my own Words*, compiled by José Louis Gonzales-Balado, Gramercy Books, a division of Random House Value Publishing, 1997, p. 21.

and He looks at me."[14] Action and contemplation support each other in the same ardent look. They are the Martha and Mary of the Gospels. "Our life and our contemplation are one. It is not a question of doing but being. In fact, it is the Holy Spirit who acts in us and inspires in us the fullness of God and sends us forth to the whole of His creation as His personal message of love."[15]

Everything is unified in this love of Christ. "My secret is infinitely simple — I PRAY. Through prayer I become one with the love of Christ. I understand deeply that to pray is to love Him."[16] She particularly insisted on silence during prayer. She always stated that the fruitfulness of her actions and that of her sisters came from their daily adoration before the Blessed Sacrament.

Blessed Mother Teresa shared the secret of prayer with the people who came to her for advice. One such encounter is told to us by Father Henri Nouwen, former chaplain of *l'Arche* (a community of faith and lifelong homes with people who have developmental disabilities) of Toronto, who died unexpectedly in September 1996. He testified that Blessed Mother Teresa always responded to a question "from below" with an answer "from above":

> One day, several years ago, I had the opportunity to meet Mother Teresa of Calcutta. At the time I was struggling with so many problems that I asked her for advice. Immediately she sat down with me, and I started to share with her all my problems and difficulties — trying to convince her that my situation was really very difficult. After ten minutes of detailed explanations, I stopped talking and was silent. Mother Teresa looked at me calmly and said: "Well, if you would sacrifice one hour of your day in adoration of your Lord,

---

14 Mother Teresa, *No Greater Love...*, p. 7.
15 *Ibid.*, p. 13.
16 *Ibid.*, p. 3.

and if you would do nothing that you don't really know how to do... everything will work out fine!"[17]

On January 15, 1973, Mother Teresa gave an interview for a scholarly program with the BBC entitled: "Faith and Life." Her answers appeared to come "from above." In a series of questions, she was asked:

Interviewer: What is the biggest obstacle you encounter in your work?

Mother Teresa: That I am not yet a saint.

Interviewer: What worries you the most when you travel around the world?

Mother Teresa: Not to be capable to fully reach out and reflect the love of Christ, because God wants that those who belong to Him be happy and holy.[18]

The Mission of Love

In a world that was more and more complicated, where knowledge upstaged wisdom, everything appeared to be very simple for Blessed Mother Teresa. This simplicity steeped in humility attracted the crowds to her. In Blessed Mother Teresa, the people recognized what is the best in themselves. Everywhere she went she brought more of her soul. Mother's simplicity manifested itself in gentleness, but a gentleness coming from an incredible source of strength. A simplicity, which places all in the hands of Providence and expects everything from it, and a divine simplicity because she was close to God who is Love. The Desert Fathers said that the more we approach God the more everything becomes simple in us and the more our prayer is simplified. A look

---

17 Henri Nouwen, *Vivre sa foi au quoditien* [*To Live One's Faith in the Everyday.* Not translated.], Montréal, Novalis, 1996, p. 97.

18 Mother Teresa, *Nous soyons jugés sur L'amour*, p. 136.

at the photographs of Blessed Mother Teresa and St. Thérèse, makes us realize that there is no need for long treatises on prayer; even less on talks about love.

Father Joseph Langford, Co-founder with Mother Teresa of the branch of priests of the Missionaries of Charity, revealed in a homily in her presence on October 1, 1984, the influence of St. Thérèse in the life of Mother Teresa. He showed that the experience of the thirst of Jesus, the vocation of being love, and the "Little Way" of confidence, were the principal elements connecting the two Theresas. Blessed Mother Teresa asked him to write and print this homily and distribute it among all the members of the congregation. Here are excerpts:

> Mother Teresa has always understood her vocation as modeled on her patron saint, St. Thérèse of Lisieux....
> St. Thérèse intuitively felt that the infinite desire of the Lord to love and to be loved by His people — which was the foundation of her little way of confidence, abandonment and love, as well as her insatiable zeal to increase divine love in souls — had its origin and source in the mystery of the thirst of Jesus. Like Mother Teresa, one rarely speaks about this hidden source (because of its indescribable and intimate nature), although it nourishes and explains profoundly and continuously the life and spirituality of St. Thérèse and Mother Teresa.
>
> The thirst of Jesus, His thirst for love and for souls is one of the reasons, if not the only reason, for the mission and the extraordinary significance of St. Thérèse. And it is this thirst, which explains the vocation of Mother Teresa.
>
> The second major connection between Mother Teresa and St. Thérèse was their call "to be love" in the Church: ...what was hidden and implicit in Mother Teresa (for example the message of love), was evident

and explicit in St. Thérèse; ...what was hidden and implicit in St. Thérèse (for example the mission of love) was evident in Mother Teresa.[19]

In order to live this mission of love the two Theresas have taken Mary as their model. Through Mary, the Unspeakable can be heard, the Invisible can be seen, the Untouchable can be touched, and the Inaccessible can be reached. As Mary has given Jesus to the world and continues to deliver Him to the Church, the two Theresas have brought Jesus into the world and have desired to be love in the heart of the Church. In this image they draw from the source of life, the Eucharist: "I am the Bread of Life. Whoever comes to me will never be hungry, whoever believes in me will never be thirsty.... Whoever eats of this bread will live forever.... Those who eat my flesh and drink my blood have eternal life and I will raise them up on the last day" (Jn 6:35, 51, 54). Mother Teresa commented: "He made Himself the bread of life to satisfy our hunger for God, then He transformed Himself into one of the starving so we can satisfy His hunger."[20]

Mother Teresa said that the greatest illnesses that people suffer from are a lack of love and loneliness, so she wanted to quench this thirst by touching the poorest of the poor as if she were touching Jesus Himself. For her, love was a fruit always in season. In giving love at any minute, any hour, she quenched the love of Jesus. Her happiness was to help the most vulnerable people of society and to touch Jesus in caring for them.

Holiness for Everyone

Mother Teresa received several international prizes, among them the 1979 Nobel Prize for Peace, which she accepted in the

---

[19] Joseph Langford, "D'une Thérèse à l'autre," pp. 38-45.
[20] Mother Teresa, *Nous serons jugés sur l'amour*, p. 148.

name of the poor. In spite of health problems, she was re-elected Superior General of the Congregation in 1990. She was hospitalized several times and lived a life of faith more and more in darkness, lasting throughout her final years. However, both Theresas were joined intimately in experiencing the joy of love in spite of physical and emotional pain.

> A woman who lived very close to Mother Teresa for several months testified: "I tell you that the presence of Mother Teresa replaces the Lord… on His altar, in this human tabernacle is His motherly heart. One experienced the entire Sacred Liturgy just by looking at her!" A volunteer who worked with me at the House of the Dying said to me: "The Lord will forgive me if during the adoration of the Blessed Sacrament, my eyes do not leave Mother Teresa. She is a true monstrance."[21]

Blessed Mother Teresa had the audacity of the builders of civilizations, which many holy women became. In her heart rushed the blood of Christ. She worked with such evangelical "violence" that there was no time left for rest. We cannot place her in a political landscape of right or left, and she was neither a fundamentalist nor a progressive. She belongs to that group of saints in Scripture who made history in a different way. Her vocation and her mission surpassed a certain historical moment. She transcended time — she is for all times.

On September 5, 1997 at the age of 87, Blessed Mother Teresa, a beautiful living symbol of merciful love died in Calcutta, India. At the end she had humbly asked whether her used sandals could be taken off her feet so that she would be able to present herself barefoot before her Lord, like St. Thérèse who had asked to present herself to Christ with "empty hands." Jacques Chirac,

---

[21] Thérèse Beaudry, *Séjour chez Mère Teresa* [*Spending Time in the Presence of Mother Teresa*. Not translated.], Montréal, Meridien, 1988, p. 51.

the President of France summed up the general reaction to Blessed Mother Teresa's death very well when he said: "Tonight, there is less love in the world, less compassion, less light." She left behind 4,000 sisters, as well as 550 priests and brothers. The Missionaries of Charity are spread over 517 missions in 120 countries.

At the midday Angelus on September 7, 1997, Pope John Paul II recalled her life: "Her mission started at sunset before the Blessed Sacrament. In the silence of contemplation Mother Teresa heard Jesus cry out, *I Thirst*, resounding from the Cross. This cry, preserved in the depth of her heart, called her to the streets of Calcutta and all the slums of the world in search of Jesus among the poor, the abandoned, and the dying. Mother Teresa, the unforgettable *Mother of the Poor* is an eloquent example for everyone." It does not seem a coincidence that only one month and a half later, on October 19, 1997 the Pope proclaimed St. Thérèse of Lisieux, a Doctor of the Church.

Mother Teresa recalled this "thirst of Jesus" in her moving *Spiritual Testament* [Appendix 2] in which she states: "The thirst of Jesus is the home, the point of convergence, and the goal of all that the Missionaries of Charity are and do. The Church has confirmed this several times: 'In our work for the salvation and sanctification of the poorest of the poor, our call is to quench the thirst of Jesus, His thirst of love for souls.' This is it and there is nothing more. Let us do everything we can to protect this gift from God to our Congregation."

This frail little woman (4' 9") started her mission in Calcutta one year after the death of Gandhi (1869-1948). India has given to the world two powerful instruments of peace: Mahatma Gandhi and Blessed Mother Teresa, two fragile creatures who lifted up the world with the lever of peace. And the joy of love became their sole support.

Blessed Mother Teresa who said that holiness was not a luxury destined for the elite but a simple task for everyone, was beatified in Rome on October 19, 2003, World Mission Day. It was also the sixth anniversary of the proclamation of St. Thérèse of Lisieux as a Doctor of the Church. The two Theresas now spend their heaven helping us on earth and guiding us to Christ.

Letter of Pope John Paul II to the Missionaries of Charity

Pope John Paul II wrote a beautiful letter to Sister Mary Nirmala Joshi, General Superior of the Congregation of the Missionaries of Charity, on the occasion of the Fiftieth Anniversary of their foundation. The letter, dated October 2, 2000, reiterates the essence of the charisma of their foundress. The following are extracts from his letter:

> In this year of the Great Jubilee, while the Church throughout the world sings the praises of the Holy Trinity for the ineffable gift of the Word made flesh, there is for you and the entire family born of the charism of Mother Teresa of Calcutta, the added joy of celebrating the 50th anniversary of the foundation of the Missionaries of Charity.
>
> It was on October 7, 1950 in the little chapel at 14 Creek Lane in Calcutta that Archbishop Ferdinand Périer established the foundress and her first 11 companions as a religious congregation of diocesan right. This moment of grace came after a long process of discernment of God's will by Mother Teresa, as she listened to the "call within a call." That small beginning has become an abundant stream of grace within the Church as the Missionaries of Charity have grown in ways that could not have been foreseen 50 years ago. For that great gift, I join you in giving glory to our heavenly Father and I exhort you in the words of the First Letter of Peter: "As each has received a gift, em-

ploy it for one another, as good stewards of God's varied grace" (4:10).

Just 15 years later, on February 1, 1965, Pope Paul VI granted the *Decretum laudis*[22] which established the Missionaries Sisters of Charity as a congregation of pontifical right. Since then, the Missionaries of Charity Family has produced abundant fruit, as God has raised up contemplative sisters, active and contemplative brothers, fathers, lay missionaries and the co-workers of Mother Teresa; and a great host of people — of all beliefs and none — have become involved in this work of love which has spread throughout the world under the inspiration and direction of Mother Teresa. "This is the work of the Lord, a marvel in our eyes" (Ps 117:23).

From the very first, Blessed Mother Teresa and the Missionaries of Charity were driven by the desire "to quench the infinite thirst of Jesus Christ on the Cross for love of souls.... by laboring for the salvation and sanctification of the poorest of the poor" (Letter of the Foundress). These are words which go to the heart of both *your consecration*, your "clinging to Jesus" in love, your thirsting for Him who thirsts for you, and *your mission* of joyful and wholehearted service to Jesus in the poorest of the poor, never forgetting the Lord's own words: "As you did it to one of the least of these, my brethren, you did it for me" (Mt 25:40). This is, as Pope Paul VI said in awarding the John XXIII Peace Prize to Mother Teresa in 1971, "the mystical and evangelical motive that transfigures the countenance of a poor, hungry person, a sickly child, someone repulsive with leprosy, or a feeble man on his deathbed, into the mysterious countenance of Christ."

---

[22] Decree of praise/papal approbation.

CHAPTER THREE

I Thirst — Give Me to Drink

"I thirst," the cry of Christ on the Cross is known to all of us. He was also thirsty when He met the Samaritan woman. St. John in his Gospel was the only Evangelist who reported this story of the Samaritan woman, especially recommended by the Church for those who are preparing for baptism. The Evangelist knew the geography and the customs of the Samaritans very well, but the story mainly serves to introduce a very specific teaching about the thirst of Jesus. The scene develops in three stages:

- the well
- the husband of the Samaritan woman
- the Samaritan people who started to believe

Let us look at the Gospel with an understanding of these three elements:

At the Well

Jesus came to Sychar, a town in the Province of Samaria, close to the property that Jacob had given to his son Joseph and Jacob's well was there. Jesus, tired from His journey, sat down at the well about noon. A

Samaritan woman came to draw water. Jesus said to her, "Give me to drink." His disciples had gone into the town to buy food. The Samaritan woman said to Him, "How can you, a Jew, ask me a Samaritan woman for a drink?" The Jews did not use anything in common with Samaritans.

Jesus answered her, "If you knew the gift of God and who it is who is saying to you, 'Give me to drink,' you would have asked Him and He would have given you living water." The woman said to Him, "Sir, you do not even have a bucket and the well is deep; where then can you get this living water? Are you greater than our father Jacob, who gave us this well and drank from it himself with his children and his flocks?"

Jesus answered and said to her, "Everyone who drinks this water will be thirsty again; but whoever drinks the water I shall give will never thirst; the water I shall give will become in him a living source of water leading to eternal life." The woman said to Him, "Sir, give me this water, so that I may not be thirsty or have to keep coming here to draw water" (Jn 4:5-15).

This gospel tells the story of an encounter of two desires and two perspectives: the one of Jesus and the one of the Samaritan woman. It is an encounter which touches the hearts of both of them, a symbol of the inner well to which we are called to drink the living water. Jesus will, in spite of the ethnic inappropriateness, reveal to the woman the truth which lies deep within her. His words will move her from her superficial ideas to the depths of her feelings. Her perception of herself will change; and she will see herself as Jesus sees her. This revelation will be her transformation. St. Thérèse recalls the meeting with Jesus and the Samaritan woman in her long poem entitled: "Jesus, My Beloved, Remember!" (PN 24, 10).

Remember that alongside the fountain
A Traveler tired by the journey
Made waves of love from within His breast
Overflow on the Samaritan woman.
Ah! I know Him who asked for a drink.
He is the Gift of God, the source of glory.
He is Water springing up.
It's He who said to us,
"Come to me."[1]

Jesus reveals to the Samaritan woman her dignity as a child of God. Blessed Mother Teresa often repeated that a person is mainly thirsting for dignity. It is love that brings a person to life in the eyes of others. These words of Mother Teresa could very well be applied to this encounter of Jesus and the Samaritan woman or with all of us:

Hungry for love, He looks at you.
Thirsty for kindness, He begs from you.
Lacking in faithfulness, He hopes in you.
Sick and deprived of friendship, He wants from you.
Homeless, desiring of shelter in your heart, He asks of you.
Will you be that one to Him?[2]

Jesus travels through Samaria, a region considered impure for the Jews. Tired and thirsty He stops at midday at the well of Jacob. This place is not just an ordinary place. In the Semitic tradition, the well is a place of life; the women come here to fetch water (Gn 24:13). The song of the squeaking wheel mingles with their laughter when they pull the water up from the depth of the

---

[1]   *The Poetry of Saint Thérèse of Lisieux*, translated by Donald Kinney, O.C.D., ICS Publications, Washington, DC, 1996, p. 125.

[2]   Mother Teresa, *No Greater Love...*, p. 86.

well. It is a privileged place for courting, as it was for Jacob and
Rachel (Gn 29).

"When there is a little beauty in the desert, it is because there
is a well hidden somewhere," said the Little Prince, who always
tried to understand with the heart that which is invisible to the
eyes. Saint-Exupéry, who carried in his wallet a photograph of St.
Thérèse of Lisieux, searched all his life for this water able to quench
his thirst for the absolute and for the silence of love.

"'I am thirsty for that water,' says the little Prince. 'Give me
to drink….' And then I understood what he was searching for! I
lifted the bucket to his lips. He drank with his eyes closed. It was
sweet like a feast. This water was not ordinary nourishment. It
was born by stages under the stars, from the chant of the pulley,
from the effort of my hands. It was good for the heart like a gift."[3]

The Gift of God

In the Gospel of St. John (4:1-27) Jesus showed us that when
He was thirsty, He went beyond preconceived ideas and religious
prejudices and asked a woman for water, revealing His need and
weakness. This Samaritan woman from Sychar came alone to the
well in the middle of the day. Normally the women came here
together with other women to get water, very early in the morning or later in the evening, but not at high noon when the sun
was at its hottest. Nevertheless, Jesus needed her to get water for
Him because He did not have the wherewithal to draw the water
from the well. It may well be that in His night prayer to the Father He may have already expressed His real desire in the formula:
"Give me to drink."

---

[3]   Antoine de Saint-Exupéry, *The Little Prince*, translated by Richard Howard, Harcourt,
Orlando, FL, p. 71.

The woman, at first, did not respond to His request. She felt unsettled by the man speaking to her. She refused to give Him to drink because Samaritans had no contact with Jews. It would be unthinkable to eat from the same plate or drink from the same cup, for such was thought to make them unclean. The Samaritans had their own version of the Pentateuch, which includes only the first five books of the Old Testament, and rejected all the rest. Had the Samaritan woman remained intolerant, it would have resulted in Jesus' remaining thirsty until the end of the story.

The Samaritan woman was most likely ashamed because she had had five husbands and was now living with another man. She had probably been called every name in the book and had been marginalized from her community which no longer showed her any respect. Jesus, however, kept taking the initiative, setting aside all discrimination, and changed the subject of the conversation completely. Jesus answered her, "If you knew the gift of God and who it is who is saying to you, 'Give me to drink,' you would have asked Him and He would have given you living water" (Jn 4:10). This obscure phrase revealed that there was a direct connection between the gift of God and that Man who spoke to her. It is He who would satisfy her thirst and not with some stagnant water but with living water. The notion of a well was being changed. This Jew defined Himself as a new well, the gift of God.

The woman's viewpoint started to change. She let herself be swept along in this special universe of His, and she then began to call Him, "Sir." She let Him know that the well was deep and that He lacked a container for the water. Where did He expect to get this living water? Jesus answered her by pointing out the parallel between her physical need for water and her spiritual thirst. His response to her was addressed to all of us. He said to her, "Everyone who drinks this water will be thirsty again; but whoever drinks the water I shall give will never thirst; the water I shall give will become in him a living source of water leading to eternal life" (Jn 4:5-14).

The dialogue was on such an elevated level that the woman was ready to receive the water which was to purify her point of view and prepare her to know herself. This is because the well of the human heart is bottomless. "Our desire can never be satisfied," St. Teresa of Avila said. St. Thérèse of Lisieux, recalling St. John of the Cross, used to like to repeat that we receive as much as we ask depending on the measure of our thirst. Our desire is our prayer. Our thirst is our search. Our prayer determines our fruitfulness if it comes from the heart. Blessed Mother Teresa said: "In order to be fruitful, our prayer must come from the heart and be able to touch the heart of God."[4] In fact, this is how the statement of the Samaritan woman, "Sir, give me this water so that I may never be thirsty or have to keep coming here to draw water" (Jn 4:15), was understood by the great mystics.

Jesus is "the master of desire"[5] who awakens in others His deep desire. "Let anyone who is thirsty come to me, and let the one who believes in me drink" (Jn 7:37). Jesus, who is the source of Living Water, desires to give of Himself so much that He even gave His body and His blood: "He said to them, 'With what longing have I longed to eat this Passover with you before I suffer'" (Lk 22:15).

In his Papal Letter entitled *Ecclesia in America* [*The Church in America*, 1999], John Paul II invited America to encounter the Living Christ. In the first chapter, he recalled with St. Augustine the thirst of Jesus, which also has a mystical meaning. Jesus asked her to quench His thirst, not only a physical thirst but "the one who needed to drink was asking rather for the faith of that woman" (St. Augustine). In telling her, "Give me to drink" (Jn 4:7), and by talking to her about living water, the Lord created within the Samaritan woman a demand, almost a prayer, which in its deeper

---

4   Mother Teresa, *No Greater Love...*, p. 15
5   Françoise Dolto, 1908-1988, French child psychoanalyst, co-founder of the French Psychoanalytic Society.

meaning and its true purpose went beyond her understanding at that moment (Jn 4:4-42).

In the Preface of the Eucharistic Prayer for the Third Sunday of Lent, the Church reminds us of Jesus' desire to awaken faith in everyone and give birth to love as He did in the case of the Samaritan woman. "When he asked the woman of Samaria for water to drink, Christ had already prepared for her the gift of faith. In His thirst to receive her faith, He awakened in her heart the fire of Your love."

We Worship in Spirit and in Truth

Jesus said to her, "Go, call your husband, and come back." The woman answered Him, "I do not have a husband." Jesus said to her, "You are right in saying, 'I have no husband,' for you have had five husbands, and the one you have now is not your husband. What you have said is true!" The woman said to Him, "Sir, I see that you are a prophet. Our ancestors worshiped on this mountain, but you say that the place where people must worship is in Jerusalem." Jesus said to her, "Woman, believe me, the hour is coming when you will worship the Father neither on this mountain nor in Jerusalem. You worship what you do not know; we worship what we know, for salvation is from the Jews. But the hour is coming, and is now here, when the true worshiper will worship the Father in spirit and truth, for the Father seeks such as these to worship Him. God is spirit, and those who worship Him must worship in spirit and truth." The woman said to Him, "I know that Messiah (who is called Christ) is coming. When He comes, He will proclaim all things to us." Jesus said to her, "I am He, the one who is speaking to you" (Jn 4:16-20).

Jesus entered into the life of the Samaritan woman to reveal to her, her inner well. That revelation contained a call to receive the living water and a challenge to conversion. In order to be spiritually transformed, the woman needed to change her way of life. That is why Jesus asked the woman to call her husband and to return to the well. He did not scold her morally but revealed to her what was hidden. His words reconnected her to the very heart of His life, His desire and His thirst. The living water had its requirements and inspired the desire of wholeness in her, but worried her at the same time.

Maybe the Samaritan woman had tried to seduce Jesus at this hour in the middle of the day when nobody went to the well. Maybe she had found the man of her life, the one who would love her for who she really was. In moving from one man to the other, her thirst for love was still not satisfied. But here she finally found someone who restored her dignity; with Him she felt that she existed in her own right, beyond her beauty and the games of seduction.

> This woman who had five men belonged to those broken and marginalized people for whom Jesus came in particular to this world. When He looked at her, He looked with the merciful eyes of His Father. It was for her that He had taken that road to the village and waited at the well of Jacob. He came to meet her, and to reveal to her the kindness of His Father. He came to tell her that she is also loved by the Father for all eternity and to awaken in her the desire for that life whose secret He carried within Himself.[6]

---

[6] Éloi Leclerc, *Le Maître du désir* [*The Master of Desire.* t translated.], Paris, DDB, 1997, p. 63.

Jesus confronted the Samaritan woman with the most intimate vulnerability of her life. He asked her to bring her husband whom she did not have. He wanted her to realize that she was in violation of the Commandment of God, which is a gift of God. Jesus also thirsted for the salvation of the woman, and He wanted to make her a disciple. Confused again, she thought Jesus was a prophet. She agreed to look at her situation and to be open with Jesus, telling Him she did not have a husband. Her vulnerability served the truth. The tenderness of Jesus wore down her resistance. She needed it more than the water from the well.

Jesus, God's gift to humankind, offered us a *new commandment*. This commandment was not something exterior but was rather something interior to the human being. The Samaritan woman wanted to go further into her inner life because she expected everything from this quest. Her thirst was immense. She dueled with Jesus about the matter of cult. From the depths of the well she passed to the mountain top. But places have little importance when they do not lead to the heart. For Jesus, the hour had come when true worshiping would no longer be found on this or that mountain, but in spirit and in truth as St. Thérèse and Mother Teresa did. Like the law and the truth, worship must come from within. That adoration is the work of the Holy Spirit who lives permanently in each believer. True worship is that which we render to the Father through the Holy Spirit. The true sanctuary is our inner self where the Spirit dwells. Every believer is holy ground.

Jesus endlessly revives our desire in prayer. By allowing His Spirit to love us gratuitously and renew us from within, and by allowing His words to touch us and embrace our silence, we worship in spirit and in truth. "If anyone is thirsty, let him come to me and drink! Whoever believes in me, as Scripture says, 'From within him shall flow rivers of living water'" (Jn 7:37). St. Thérèse of Lisieux did nothing but that, drink the living water Jesus had offered her in the spirit of the Gospel of the Samaritan woman.

Jesus does not demand great deeds from us but simply *surrender* and *gratitude*.(…) He has no need of our works but only of our *love*, for the same God who declares He *has no need to tell us when He is hungry* did not fear to *beg* for a little water from the Samaritan Woman. He was thirsty. But when He said: "*Give me to drink,*" it was the *love* of His poor creature the Creator of the universe was seeking. He was thirsty for love. Ah! I feel it more than ever before, Jesus is *parched*, for He meets only the ungrateful and indifferent among His disciples in the world, and among *His own disciples*, alas, He finds few hearts who surrender to Him without reservations, who understand the real tenderness of His infinite Love. (MsB, 1v)[7]

Welcome the Savior of the World

When Jesus had said, "The hour will come," the Samaritan woman responded: "I know that Messiah (who is called Christ) is coming. When He comes, He will proclaim all things to us." A threshold was about to be crossed by the two who understood each other because they attentively listened to each other. The Samaritan woman shared her secret with Jesus and now He reveals His identity to her as He had never done before in John's Gospel: "I am He, the one who is speaking to you." This line reminds us of God on Mt. Sinai when He spoke of Himself saying: "I AM." The woman was ready to hear that revelation, and was able to leave the well and the jug and even the mountain behind, since all she needed had been given to her. "The woman left her water jar and went off to the city and said to the people: 'Come and see a man who told me everything I have done. Could He possibly be the

---

[7] *Story of a Soul*, p. 189.

Messiah?' They left the town and went out to him" (Jn 4:28-30).

To welcome Jesus who comes to meet us, and look for us and wants to give Himself to us, that is our apostolic vocation. To welcome Him in the poor, the weak, the rejected, the excluded, as for example, to welcome the little children during the time in which He lived, meant to welcome God: "Whoever welcomes one such child in my name welcomes Me, and whoever welcomes Me, welcomes not Me but the One who sent Me" (Mk 9:37). The "first" for Jesus is the one who serves the rest, above all the little ones. Through her life, Mother Teresa strongly proclaimed these lines of the Gospel. She only did little things but with great love, always remembering the words of St. Thérèse which originated from St. John of the Cross in his *Spiritual Canticle*: "...the smallest act of PURE LOVE *is of more value to her [the Church] than all other works together*" (MsB 4v).[8]

Our response is to humbly recognize that we need Jesus, to love Him with confidence and give ourselves fully to Him as Mother Teresa told us: "Give yourself completely to Jesus. He takes you as an instrument to accomplish wonders under the condition that you are infinitely more conscious of His love than your weakness. Believe in Him, put yourself into His hands in the spirit of blind and absolute confidence, because He is Jesus."[9]

The Samaritan woman experienced this love of Jesus and she understood His desire to give Himself. She no longer had the same kind of thirst as before, because Jesus in taking on our humanity, liberated her profound desire and showed her a source of living water which gave meaning to her life thus enabling her to abandon her life on the fringes of society. She recognized that man as the Messiah and she was finally free. Thanks to her, the story ended with this extraordinary confession of faith: "No longer do

---

[8]   *Story of a Soul*, p. 197, and St. John of the Cross, *Spiritual Canticle*, stanza 29, no. 2, *Collected Works*, p. 587.

[9]   Mother Teresa, *No Greater Love...*, p. 149.

we believe because of what you said — we've heard for ourselves and we know that this man is truly the savior of the world" (Jn 4:42).

The Samaritan woman, whose name we don't even know, became a disciple of Jesus like Mary Magdalene. She was not able to keep this Jesus, who had revealed Himself to her heart, for herself alone. It was He, Christ the Messiah, the Son of God. Her recognition of the divine presence and her faith in Him was stronger than herself. Her faith was so radiant that it became contagious, and drew the Samaritans, a whole people, to Jesus, a Jewish man, who had been tired and thirsty. Love gives you wings, St. Thérèse tells us: "With love not only did I advance, I actually *flew*" (MsA 80v).[10] St. Thérèse liked the words from the Canticle of Canticles (the Song of Songs) which applied very well to the Samaritan woman: "Your anointing oils are fragrant, your name is perfume poured out; therefore the maidens love you. Draw me after you, let us make haste" (Sg 1:3-4).

> I understand, Lord, that when a soul allows herself to be captivated by *the odor of your ointments*, she cannot run alone, all the souls whom she loves follow in her train; this is done without constraint, without effort, it is a natural consequence of her attraction for You. Just as a torrent, throwing itself with impetuosity into the ocean, drags after it everything it encounters in its passage, in the same way, O Jesus, the soul who plunges into the shoreless ocean of Your Love, draws with her all the treasures she possesses. Lord, You know it, I have no other treasures than the souls it has pleased You to unite to mine... (MsC, 34r).[11]

---

[10] *Story of a Soul*, p. 174.

[11] *Ibid.*, p. 254.

The Living Water of Prayer

Other women will meet Jesus and will equally quench His thirst in the same amazing relationship, as our two Theresas have done. And there was also a third Teresa who was inspired by the Samaritan woman to discover the living water of prayer, St. Teresa of Avila. The Carmel of Lisieux was strongly influenced by the reformer of Carmel. For Mother Teresa this influence was significant in her prayer life.

"We call mental prayer the one that comes from both the intelligence and the heart. We must never forget that we are destined for perfection and that we can never stop searching for it. The daily practice of mental prayer is indispensable for that purpose. Because it is the vital breath which permeates our soul, holiness is impossible without it. Mental prayer grows the more we become simple, the more we let go of selfishness, the more we go beyond the physical and the senses and renew our aspirations which nourish our prayer. During our vocal prayer, we speak to God; during mental prayer, God speaks to us. It is at this moment that He unites Himself to us."[12]

St. Teresa of Avila used the symbol of water to illustrate a progression during prayer. The request of the Samaritan woman for water changed her whole life to one single desire: "Lord, give me that water" (Jn 4:15). In order to receive the living water of contemplation, St. Teresa, an excellent teacher, discovered four different ways to water the garden of her soul. They were also called degrees or stages in mental prayer.

First Stage: MEDITATION. "The persons who start to pray are pulling water from the deep well and it is hard work, I have pointed that out already. Therefore, they need to make extraordinary efforts to recollect their senses which are accustomed to focus on the exterior.... It is the life of Christ they need to be

---

[12] Mother Teresa, *No Greater Love...*, p. 15.

43

occupied with and that exercise is a challenge to our understanding which is tiring." (*Book of Life* 11, 9)

Second Stage: CONTEMPLATION. "As the soul starts to enter into contemplation, she touches on the supernatural. It is clear that whatever her efforts, it is impossible to achieve on her own what happens now.... The will finds itself captivated and, without knowing how it happened, imprisoned by God, totally reassured of falling into the power of the One she loves." (*Book of Life* 14, 1-2)

Third Stage: TRANQUILITY. "This prayer seems void of all personal powers, as if in a sleep in which, without being completely suspended, they simply do not understand how they are working.... The soul is so entirely plunged into the floods of grace, that she is unable to either move backwards or forward or even see at all: she only longs to rejoice in her happiness." (*Book of Life* 16,1)

Fourth Stage: UNION. "May the Lord teach me the right words to describe the fourth water!... This water which falls from heaven, falls often at the moment when the gardener least expects it. In the beginning, it is true, it is almost always after a long mental prayer." (*Book of Life* 18,1,9) "Here it is love embracing love." (*The Interior Castle* V,4,3)

St. Thérèse of Lisieux and Blessed Mother Teresa became the prayerful souls who drew from the source of the living water of which St. Teresa of Avila was speaking. It is here that we must search for the secret of their fruitfulness. In spite of their silent prayer which most often was arid, they asked in faithfulness for water and they quenched the thirst of Jesus, in opening up to His desire to unite them to His cry on the Cross: "I thirst." The desire of God became flesh in this cry of Jesus.

The three Theresas heard the cry of Jesus' desire and made it their own. "For the love of Christ urges us on" (2 Cor 14). God manifested His desire by awaking in these women their desire for Him. They entered into this adventure of God's desire by drawing on their own experiences. They understood from deep within that "the person who experiences a great desire in his heart for God has also understood that it is God Himself who is completely saturated by an infinite desire for His creature."[13]

Prayer of the Japanese Cooperators of Mother Teresa

Oh! Lord,
When I am hungry,
Give me someone who is in need of nourishment.
When I am thirsty, someone who needs water.
When I am cold, send me someone whom I can give
    warmth.
When I am hurt, give me someone to console.

When my cross becomes heavy, give me the cross of
    someone else to share.
When I am poor, guide me to someone in need.
When I don't have the time, send me someone whom I
    can help for a moment.
When I am humiliated, send me someone whom I can
    praise.
When I am discouraged, send me someone to encourage.
When I am in need to understand others, give me
    someone who needs my understanding.
When I need someone to take care of me, send me
    someone who I can take care of.
When I think of myself only, turn my thoughts to others.

---

[13]   Hubert Debbasch, *L'Homme de désir, icône de Dieu* [*Man of Desire, Icon of God*. Not translated.], Paris, Beauchesne, 2001, p. 101.

CHAPTER FOUR

"Amen, I say to you, whatever you did for one of these least brothers of mine, you did for me"

God is first and foremost Merciful Love. St. Thérèse and Blessed Mother Teresa were deeply inspired to believe that His compassion sprang from His mercy. They cared for the suffering in others with great tenderness, knowing that we are all people who are wounded, vulnerable and fragile. They responded to the pain of humankind by carrying it in their hearts. From their strong identification with the Merciful Love of Jesus, emerged their totally gratuitous gift of self in the service of others. This is the dynamic of true engagement, which beautifully brings us back to the Parable of the Good Samaritan (Lk 10:29-37).

The Good Samaritan

Several Church Fathers have seen in the Good Samaritan, Jesus Himself, who reached down to a deeply wounded humanity, attending to their wounds, and bringing them to shelter, which they saw as the image of the Church. The expression, "moved by compassion," used by St. Luke in this Parable, is applied only to Jesus in the New Testament. We encounter this feeling of Jesus again when He was before the crowds who were lonely, deeply troubled, abandoned and in desperate need of a shepherd (Mt 9:36), when He met the blind man of Jericho who cried out in pain (Mt 20:34), when He met the widow of Naïn who buried her only son (Lk 7:11-17), and when He met the lepers who were excluded from the community (Lk 17:11-19). Jesus was so deeply "moved by compassion" (Mt 14:14) whenever He encountered people, including children in the crowd who were sick, lost, abandoned and desperate, that He was unable to hold Himself back from showing His compassion. Thus, He took up their burden and acted to relieve their suffering and save their lives. God has but one desire — to save souls. This desire overflows from His Merciful and Trinitarian love. In the divine dynamic of Trinitarian love, the Father gives Himself to the Son, the Son receives that overflow of immense love which gives birth to the Spirit, who is the joy of both the Father and the Son. This essential movement of the Trinity, "compels God to reach out, thus allowing Him to find His joy in the complete giving of Himself. God's happiness is measured by the extent to which He is able to amplify His love."[1] That includes even, for example, giving a glass of water out of love: "Whoever gives you a cup of water to drink because you bear the name of Christ, will by no means lose the reward" (Mk 9:41).

Blessed Mother Teresa became the living realization of that message. "The neighbor who always needs me the most is the one in my own household," she used to repeat over and over again. She invited everyone to share in the needs of one's own vicinity, out of faithfulness to Christ, by helping one person at a time: a smile, a visit, a helping hand, a glass of water.... "In your own home you have a Christ who is starving, a Christ who is naked, a Christ who is without shelter. Are you able to recognize Him?"[2]

---

[1] Louis Menvielle, *Thérèse Docteur racontée par le Père Marie-Eugène de L'Enfant Jésus*, Tome II, *Les clés de la Petite Voie* [*Thérèse as Doctor, explained by Father Marie-Eugène of the Child Jesus*, Vol. II, *The keys to the Little Way*. Not translated.], Venasque et Saint-Maure, Éd. du Carmel et Éd. Parole et Silence, 1998, p. 66.

[2] Mother Teresa, *We Will be Judged on Love*, p. 32.

The Beggar of Love

Jesus is present in the person who is thirsty and wounded, who waits for a "good Samaritan." Who will bring Him relief? St. Thérèse of Lisieux saw God as a beggar who is thirsty, who asks for our "yes," and puts Himself at our mercy as He did with Mary, the one who responded in this way to all annunciations. He begs for our love and our freely committed "yes" because He needs us.

> He made Himself poor so we might be able to give Him love. He holds out His hand to us like a *beggar* so that on the radiant day of judgment when He will appear in His glory, He may let us hear those sweet words: "Come, blessed of my Father, for I was hungry and you gave me to eat; I was thirsty, and you gave me to drink"; (…) it is He who wants our love, who *begs* for it…. He places Himself, so to speak, at our mercy, He does not want to take anything unless we give it to Him (LT 145).[3]

In fact, in this is our own suffering. God does not wait for us to offer Him our suffering, but for us to become like Him who suffers. It seems to me that God is very like us in the face of suffering, that is to say, in His helplessness, powerlessness, and vulnerability. He fully renounces His power not to prevent us from suffering. Instead, He suffers with us because He respects our liberty and freedom. He suffers seeing us suffer because He is Love, just as He rejoices when He sees our maladies overcome.

However, those who say "yes" to His Cross, discover an extraordinary fruitfulness on the supernatural plane. Jesus Himself, the Christ, the equal of God, stripped Himself completely in tak-

---

[3] *Letters*, vol. II, p. 808.

ing on our mortal human condition. He even humbled Himself unto death on the Cross. For this reason "God highly exalted Him and gave Him the name that is above every name," as Saint Paul wrote in his Letter to the Philippians (Ph 2:9). Some Christian mystics who have experienced the stigmata testify to this mysterious fruitfulness of the Cross. St. Thérèse and Blessed Mother Teresa are in a long line of friends of Jesus who have sought to console Him by quenching His thirst for souls with an active and redemptive love.

St. Thérèse wrote to her sister Céline: "Jesus wills that the salvation *of souls* depends on the sacrifices of our love. He is begging for souls from us…. Ah, let us understand His *gaze!* There are so few who understand it…. Let us make our life a continual sacrifice, a martyrdom of love, in order to console Jesus. He wants only a *look, a sigh,* but a look and a sigh that are for *Him alone!*" (LT 96).[4] She picked up that theme the following year: "He has so much *need of love* and He is *so thirsty,* that He expects from us the drop of water that must refresh Him! Ah! let us give without counting the cost. One day, He will say, 'Now, my turn'" (LT 107).[5]

To Help God

During the Holocaust of World War II, the systematic extermination of the Jews, another young woman understood, in her own way, that God needs us. Etty Hillesum, a 29-year-old Jewish woman from Amsterdam, died in November 1943 in Auschwitz, Poland. She left a very moving diary in which the reader becomes a witness to her total spiritual transformation — her awareness that her life and impending death are a gift of herself

---

4   *Letters*, vol. I, p. 588.
5   *Letters*, vol. I, p. 622.

to others. The book ends with these words: "We should be willing to act as a balm for all wounds."[6] Her spiritual ascent is astonishing because it is God who progressively drew her to His thirst. She drew from the rich inner source in her heart where God lived. There she went down on her knees in profound adoration to allow the living water of compassion to well up. She was confident that she could help God and tried to transform every human home, every human heart into a sanctuary for Him: "And I promise You, yes, I promise that I shall find a dwelling and a refuge for You in as many homes as possible. There are so many empty houses, which I shall prepare for You, where You will be received as the most honored guest."[7]

When the agonies of a suffering humanity crossed her own life, the realization that the Nazis were systematically killing the Jews in the gas chambers of the concentration camps, Etty's faith in life and in God never weakened. "Life is essentially good; and when things go awry sometimes, it's not God's fault but our own. That's what remains with me, even now, as I am about to be packed off to Poland with my whole family."[8]

She wrote this beautiful prayer of compassion one Sunday morning:

> Dear God. These are anxious times. Tonight for the first time I lie in the dark with burning eyes as scene after scene of human suffering passes before me. I promise You one thing, God, just one very small thing: I shall never burden my today with cares about tomorrow, although that takes some practice. Each day is sufficient unto itself. I will try to help You, my God, to keep You alive in me, but I can't guarantee in ad-

---

6   Etty Hillesum, *An Interrupted Life*, Henry Holt and Company Publishers, New York, 1996, p. 231.

7   *Ibid.*, p. 205.

8   *Ibid.*, p. 281.

vance that I will succeed. One thing is becoming increasingly clearer to me: that You cannot help us, that we must help You to help us. God, all we can manage these days and all that really matters, is that we protect that little piece of You in ourselves, and perhaps in others as well.[9]

The Least Among My People

God is looking for friends so that His heart, burning with love can expand. He delights in His children, above all the weakest, the most destitute, because they need His love the most. St. Thérèse and Blessed Mother Teresa became real friends of God by giving relief to the most destitute and by that very fact, to God Himself. "Amen, I say to you, whatever you have done to the least brothers of mine you have done to me" (Mt 25:40).

These words, drawn from the scene of the Last Judgment, remind us not only of the Gospel of St. Matthew, but also of the lives of our two Theresas. From their spirituality the following three ideas can be extracted:

(1) To do the little things of daily life with great love for the people who live in our immediate world.

(2) To love above all, the least and the poorest in the name of Jesus.

(3) To give all to Jesus who thirsts for our love.

Blessed Mother Teresa wrote:

What we need is to love without exhausting ourselves. How does a lamp burn? By the consumption of steadily dripping drops of oil. What are the drops of oil in our own lamps? The little things in daily life: faithfulness,

---

[9] *Ibid.*, p. 178.

a friendly word, a kind thought for others, to remain silent instead of arguing or defending oneself, attentiveness to others, and honesty and strength to speak and act when necessary. Do not search for Jesus far from you. He is not somewhere else, He is in you. Keep your lamp burning and you will recognize Him.[10]

The mystique of St. Thérèse and Blessed Mother Teresa is a mystique of action, which flows from their desire for God and their will to love especially in the dark night of their faith. Blessed Jan Van Ruusbroec, a 15th century Dutch mystic is quoted as saying: A mystic is one who "hungers and thirsts," who has "a strong, incessant passion born of a feeling of constant deprivation, because all love yearns for God, desires God and longs to be touched by Him."[11]

For St. Thérèse who lived in Carmel, this desire to love was manifested in the search for "imperfect souls" around her, those with chronic emotional weaknesses, as she wrote to her Prioress Mother Marie de Gonzague in Manuscript C at the end of her life when she only had four months left to live.

> When I speak of imperfect souls, I don't want to speak of spiritual imperfections since the most holy souls will be perfect only in heaven; but I want to speak of a lack of judgment, good manners, touchiness in certain characters; all these things which don't make life very agreeable. I know very well that these moral infirmities are chronic, that there is no hope of a cure, but I also know that my Mother would not cease to take care of me, to try to console me, if I remained sick all my life. This is

---

[10] Mother Teresa, *No Greater Love...*, p. 22.
[11] Herwig Arts, "To Hunger and Thirst for God — A Spirituality of Desire," in *Communio*, International Catholic Review, Washington, DC, September/October 1990, p. 103.

the conclusion I draw from this: I must seek out in recreation, on free days, the company of Sisters who are the least agreeable to me in order to carry out with regard to these wounded souls the office of the good Samaritan. A word, an amiable smile, often suffice to make a sad soul bloom; but it is not principally to attain this end that I wish to practice charity, for I know I would soon become discouraged: a word I shall say with the best intention will perhaps be interpreted wrongly. Also, not to waste my time, I want to be friendly with everybody (and especially with the least amiable Sisters) to give joy to Jesus (MsC 28r-28v).[12]

Blessed Mother Teresa often quoted the text of the Last Judgment in the Gospel of St. Matthew in her numerous conferences and in her texts. "Christ starved Himself to satisfy His love for me, to offer me the occasion to nourish Him in the one who is hungry, to clothe Him in the one who is naked and to care for Him in the one who is sick, to give Him shelter in the homeless. This is what transforms each Missionary of Charity into a contemplative in the middle of the world. When we are able to touch Jesus in the poor, we have the possibility of remaining in His presence all day long."[13]

Let us meditate on the following text from the Gospel of St. Matthew about the true practice of Christian life which has profoundly marked the two Theresas:

> Then the king will say to those at His right hand, "Come, you who are blessed by My Father, inherit the kingdom prepared for you from the foundation of the world; for I was hungry and you gave Me food, I was thirsty and you gave Me something to drink, I was a

---

12 *Story of a Soul*, p. 246.
13 Mother Teresa, *We Will be Judged on Love*, p. 28.

stranger and you welcomed Me, I was naked and you gave Me clothing, I was sick and you took care of Me, I was in prison and you visited Me." Then the righteous will answer Him, "Lord, when was it that we saw you hungry and gave you food, or thirsty and gave you something to drink? And when was it that we saw you a stranger and welcomed you, or naked and gave you clothing? And when was it that we saw you sick or in prison and visited you?" And the king will answer them, "Amen, I say to you, what you have done to one of the least brothers of mine, you did for Me" (Mt 25:34-40).

Two Concrete Examples

This passage from the Gospel of St. Matthew is the cornerstone on which the Missionaries of Charity were founded. They see Jesus in those who are hungry, in those who are abandoned and in those who are dying. The selfless love of the poor became the priority of Jesus, and also for Blessed Mother Teresa, because our Christian faith, which is rooted in the concrete love of neighbor, is not a theory but an action. Blessed Mother Teresa confides:

> One day I picked up a man who was lying in the gutter. His body was covered with worms. I carried him to our hospice. He did not utter any curses, he did not blame any person. Instead, he simply said: "I have lived like an animal in the street but I shall be dying like an angel, as one who had been loved and taken care of!" It took us three hours to wash him, and when we finished, the man looked at the sister who had washed him and said: "My sister, I am going back home — to God." And then he died. Never have I seen a smile so

radiant as the one I saw on the face of this man. He had gone back home — to God. See what love can accomplish! It is possible that the young sister did not think of it at the moment, but she had touched the body of Christ. Did not Jesus say: "Amen, I say to you, whatever you did for the least brothers of mine, you did for me" (Mt 25:40). It is here, at this point, that you and I are written into God's plan.[14]

The poet John Milton[15] wrote: "It is not in a place but in His heart where we live." The heart is the living place of God, the place of His presence and His thirst. Olivier Clément[16] said that "the heart is the sun, which stays inside." To live in the heart is to let oneself be loved by the God of love and to hear His cry, "I thirst." The more we allow God to love us, the better we can quench the thirst for love in others in the name of Jesus, especially the poorest of the poor. St. Thérèse told us a story, which happened to her and which illustrates how this active love is available to all of us:

> I remember an act of charity God inspired me to perform while I was still a novice. It was only a very small thing, but *our Father who sees in secret* [Lk 14:12] and who looks more upon the intention than upon the greatness of the act *has already* rewarded me without my having to wait for the next life. It was at the same time Sister St. Pierre was still going to the choir and the refectory. She was placed in front of me during evening prayer. At ten minutes to six a Sister had to

---

14 Mother Teresa, *No Greater Love...*, p. 23.

15 John Milton, 1608-1674, English poet. His most widely read book entitled *Paradise Lost*, written in 1667, was a poem about Satan's rebellion against God and the story of Adam and Eve in the Garden of Eden [trans.].

16 Olivier Clément, 1923- , founder of the Aletti Center for Dialogue between Eastern and Western Christians [trans.].

get up and lead her to the refectory, for the infirmarians had too many patients and were unable to attend to her. It cost me very much to offer myself for this little service because I knew it was not easy to please Sister St. Pierre. She was suffering very much and she did not like it when her helpers were changed. However I did not want to lose such a beautiful opportunity for exercising charity, remembering the words of Jesus: *"Whatever you do to the least of my brothers, you do to me."* I offered myself very humbly to lead her and it was with a great deal of trouble that I succeeded in having my services accepted! I finally set to work and had so much good will that I succeeded perfectly.

Each evening when I saw Sister St. Pierre shake her hourglass I knew this meant: Let's go! It is incredible how difficult it was for me to get up, especially at the beginning; however, I did it immediately, and then a ritual was set in motion, I had to remove and carry her little bench in a certain way, above all I was not to hurry, and then the walk took place. It was a question of following the poor invalid by holding her cincture; I did this with as much gentleness as possible. But if by mistake she took a false step, immediately it appeared to her that I was holding her incorrectly and that she was about to fall. "Ah! my God! You are going too fast; I am going to break something." If I tried to go more slowly: "Well, come on! I don't feel your hand; you've let me go and I am going to fall! Ah! I was right when I said you were too young to help me."

Finally we reached the refectory without mishap; and here other difficulties arose. I had to seat Sister St. Pierre and I had to act skillfully in order not to hurt her; then I had to turn back her sleeves (again in a certain way), and afterward I was free to leave. With her poor crippled hands she was trying to manage with her bread as well as she could. I soon noticed this, and, each evening, I did not leave her until after I had rendered her this little service. As she had not asked for this, she was very much touched by my attention, and it was by this means that I gained her entire good graces, and this especially (I learned this later) because, after cutting her bread for her, I gave her my most beautiful smile before leaving her all alone (MsC 28r-29v).[17]

Prayer of Mother Teresa

O Jesus, You, who suffer, grant that this day and all the days of my life, I may be able to see You in the afflicted — and in serving them, to serve You.

Grant that, even if You are hidden under the unattractive disguise of anger, of crime, or of madness, I may recognize You and say, "Jesus, You who suffer, how sweet it is to serve You."

Give me, Lord, this vision of faith, and my work will never be monotonous and I will find joy in harboring even the most modest little whims and desires of all the poor who suffer.

And you, dear ill stricken neighbor, you are still more beloved to me because you represent Christ, what a privilege I am granted in being able to serve you.

O God, since You are Jesus who suffers, deign to be for me also a Jesus who is patient, indulgent with my faults, who looks at my intentions, which are to love You and to serve You in the person of each of these children of Yours who suffer.

Lord, increase my faith. Bless my efforts and my work now and forever.[18]

---

[17] *Story of a Soul*, p. 247.
[18] Mother Teresa, *No Greater Love…*, p. 183.

CHAPTER FIVE

The Broken Heart

St. John of the Cross undoubtedly became the spiritual master of St. Thérèse of Lisieux.[1] "Ah, how many lights have I not drawn from the works of our holy Father, St. John of the Cross! At the ages of seventeen and eighteen I had no other spiritual nourishment; later on however, all books left me in aridity and I'm still in that state" (MsA 83r).[2]

When I discovered the writings of St. John of the Cross at the age of twenty-one, he also became for me, just as he had been for St. Thérèse, the guide to show me the way to union with God. It was later on that I found the same themes — listed below — in the spirituality of St. Thérèse and Blessed Mother Teresa:

- The primacy of love
- The greatness of humility
- God who thirsts to be loved
- The life of prayer
- The purgative value of suffering for love
- Fraternal charity
- The importance of holding on to God exclusively

---

[1]   Guy Gaucher, *John and Thérèse: Flames of Love*, The Influence of St. John of the Cross in the Life and Writings of St. Thérèse of Lisieux, translated by Alexandra Plettenberg-Serban, Alba House, New York, 1999.

[2]   *Story of a Soul*, p. 179.

- The will to abandon oneself
- Leaving a place inside one's heart for God
- The burning love of the Holy Spirit.[3]

The influence of St. John of the Cross on St. Thérèse is clearly evident up until her last days. She confided one month before her death: "Ah! it is incredible how all my hopes have been fulfilled. When I used to read St. John of the Cross, I begged God to work out in me what he wrote, that is, the same thing as though I were to live to be very old; to consume me rapidly in Love, and I have been answered!" (LC, 9).[4] Both St. John of the Cross and St. Thérèse, deeply in love with God, responded to the thirst of Jesus even when they were in complete spiritual darkness, soaring ever higher beyond all rational explanation toward something that the heart burns so to obtain,[5] something they were unable to put in words.

The Abandoned Shepherd

The goal of the writings of St. John of the Cross is to lead us to union with God. In order to arrive there, he recommends three means: faith, love, and the imitation of Christ. He knew from experience that the profound desire of the human being can only be fully fulfilled through union with God. All his poetry sings about this desire of the soul for God and the desire of God for the soul. This is especially manifested in a moving poetic drama

---

[3]   Jacques Gauthier, *L'experience de Dieu avec Jean de la Croix* [*The Experience of God with John of the Cross.* Not translated.], Montréal, Fídes, 1998, p. 12.

[4]   St. Thérèse of Lisieux, *Last Conversations*, translated by John Clarke, O.C.D., ICS Publications, Washington, DC, 1977, p. 177.

[5]   *The Collected Works of St. John of the Cross*, translated by Kieran Kavanaugh, O.C.D., ICS, Washington, DC, 1999, p. 72. Verses 8 and 9 express the essential theme of the soul ardently longing for God (Who is difficult to comprehend humanly speaking), but love, hope and humility draw us closer to an understanding of Him [trans.].

about a shepherd in love, who represents Christ, who is deeply hurt because His shepherdess, who represents humankind, has forgotten Him. The poem was probably written in Granada between 1584 and 1585:[6]

A Lone Young Shepherd

1. A lone young shepherd, lived in pain,
   Withdrawn from pleasure and contentment,
   His thoughts fixed on a shepherd-girl,
   His heart an open wound with love.

2. He weeps, but not from the wound of love,
   There is no pain in such affliction,
   However deeply it opens the heart;
   He weeps in knowing he has been forgotten.

3. That one thought: His shining one
   Has forgotten him, in such great pain
   That he gives himself up to brutal
   Handling in a foreign land,
   His heart an open wound with love.

4. The shepherd says: I pity the one
   Who draws himself back from my love,
   And does not seek the joy of my Presence,
   Though my heart is an open wound
   With love for him.

5. After a long time he climbed a tree,
   And spread His shining arms,
   And hung by them and died,
   His heart an open wound with love.

---

[6]   *Ibid. Stanzas Applied Spiritually to Christ and the Soul* ("A Lone Young Shepherd"), p. 57.

It would be a grave injustice to St. John of the Cross to attempt to interpret this poem, because he himself did not want to interpret or explain it, a different position from his other poetic works. He confirmed that everything was expressed in his poetry, which formed the substance of his mystical theology. We remember the words from the Prologue of *The Spiritual Canticle*: "It is better to explain the utterances of love in their broadest sense so that each one may derive profit from them according to the mode and capacity of his spirit, rather than narrow them down to a meaning unadaptable to every palate."[7] This precaution foreseen by the author, does not prevent us from reflecting and meditating on his poem in the spirit of love.

The Wound of Love

The shepherd had given His all to His shepherdess and thinks of her constantly. He was happy loving her, delighted by the eternal act of love which came directly from the heart of the Blessed Trinity. The shepherd was weeping and in excruciating pain. He was dying from a broken heart, because the beautiful shepherdess had forgotten Him and rejected His love which she considered worthless. In spurning His love, in refusing to take pleasure in His presence, she risked her own unhappiness. To see His shepherdess suffer by turning away from His love left Him heartbroken. St. John of the Cross, in his poem *The Spiritual Canticle*, used the image of the wounded stag [like the shepherd] to once again illustrate the theme of the wound of love. In his own commentary to this poem he introduced some of the meaning:

> The bridegroom in this verse compares himself to a stag. It is characteristic of the stag that he climbs to high places and when wounded races in search of refresh-

---

[7]   *Ibid.*, p. 470.

ment and cool waters. If he hears the cry of his mate and senses that she is wounded, he immediately runs to her to comfort and caress her.

The bridegroom now acts similarly. Beholding that the bride is wounded with love for him, because of her moan he also is wounded with love for her. Among lovers, the wound of the one is a wound for both, and the two have but one feeling. Thus, in other words, he says: Return to me, my bride, because if you go about wounded with love for me, I too, like the stag, will come to you wounded by your wound. Also by appearing in a high place I am like the stag.[8]

The shepherd was in pain, His heart mortally wounded, and yet He waited for a response from His shepherdess. He wished that she would share her life with Him, and that she understood His wounded heart. Love asks for reciprocity. St. Thérèse formed her concept of a relationship with Jesus out of this understanding, which she came to know in the writings of St. John of the Cross: "Love is paid by love alone" (LT 85).[9] She wrote the following in her short play, *The Divine Little Beggar of Christmas*:[10]

I know it, your soul only wants to
Console Him day and night
Well! The Pillow which He desires
Is your heart burning with love. (Play 5)

---

[8]   *Ibid.*, p. 523.

[9]   *Letters*, vol. I, p. 546.

[10] Saint Thérèse de L'Enfant-Jesus et de La Sainte-Face, *Récreations pieuses, Prières* [*Pious recreations, Prayers*], Nouvelle Édition du Centenaire, Les Édition du Cerf et Desclée De Brouwer, 1992, p. 187.

Exchange of Hearts

This broken heart, wounded out of love for us, so beautifully described in the poem of St. John of the Cross, was revealed to Margaret Mary Alacoque, a religious of the Visitation convent at Paray-le-Monial in France, between the years 1673 and 1675. In a true exchange of hearts, Jesus called her "The Beloved Disciple of My Sacred Heart."

> He made me rest for a long time on His divine breast where He showed me the marvels of His love and the unspeakable secrets of His sacred heart that had always been hidden before. He opened them to me there for the first time, in such a real and tangible way. Even though I am always afraid of deceiving myself about what I say happens inside me, I could not doubt what was happening because of the effects that the grace produced in me. This is what seemed to me to happen: He said to me, "My divine heart is so impassioned with love for humanity, and for you especially, it cannot contain the flames of its burning charity inside. It must spread them through you, and show itself to humanity so that they may be enriched by the previous treasures that I shared with you."
>
> Afterwards, He asked for my heart. I begged Him to take it and He did, placing it in His own adorable heart. He let me see it there like a little atom consumed in a burning furnace. Then He returned it to me in a burning heart-shaped flame and placed it where it had been.[11]

---

[11] Saint Margaret Mary, *Autobiography of St. Margaret Mary*, translated by the Sisters of the Visitation, Rockford, IL, TAN Books, 1968, p. 69.

It was during the main revelation in June, 1675, that Jesus said to His beloved Margaret Mary, who was 27 years old at the time:

> Behold this Heart, which has loved human kind so much, that It has spared Itself nothing, even to the point of exhausting and consuming Itself in order to show them Its love; and in return I receive from most only ingratitude through their irreverence and sacrileges as well as through the coldness and contempt in which they hold the Sacrament of Love. But what hurts me most is that those hearts who are consecrated to me so often treat me in this way.[12]

Jesus confided to St. Margaret Mary about His suffering in several different revelations. He shared with her His pain because He had been forgotten by so many, and had not been loved in return for all the love that He had given. "They are simply cold and dismissive of all my efforts to do good to them. But, at least, you please me by making up for their ingratitude to the extent that you are able."[13] Responding to St. Margaret Mary's passionate desire to receive the Eucharist more often, Jesus said to her: "My daughter, I see the ardent desire of your heart and it is so pleasing to me that if I had not already established My Sacrament of Love, I would do it out of love for you so that I would have the pleasure to rest in your soul and make My loving home in your heart."[14]

We understand that St. Thérèse was very touched by the experience of St. Margaret Mary. We find here the same desire to console Jesus because of others' ingratitude. St. Thérèse's family was very familiar with this friend of the Sacred Heart of Jesus. Léonie, the third sister of St. Thérèse, was healed in March 1865

---

[12] *Ibid.*, p. 70.

[13] *Ibid.*, p. 72.

[14] *Ibid.*, p. 72.

as a result of a novena to St. Margaret Mary. After two unsuccessful attempts to enter the convent, Léonie finally entered the Visitation Monastery in Caen in 1899, and was known to have lived an exemplary and holy life. St. Thérèse read the life of St. Margaret Mary in her Carmelite convent, and she used the image of the "atom" in her poem entitled *The Atom of the Sacred Heart*, referring to St. Margaret Mary. She confided to her sister Céline: "Pray to the Sacred Heart; you know that I myself do not see the Sacred Heart as everybody else. I think that the Heart of my Spouse is mine alone, just as mine is His alone, and so I speak to Him in the solitude of this delightful heart-to-heart, while waiting to contemplate Him one day face-to-face..." (LT 122).[15]

St. Thérèse went beyond the symbolism of the wounded heart in order to focus directly on the reality of Jesus Himself, His feelings, His love, His desire to be loved and His thirst for souls. "Let us not grow tired of prayer; confidence works miracles. And Jesus said to St. Margaret Mary: 'One just soul has so much power over my Heart that it can obtain pardon for a thousand criminals'" (LT 129).[16] St. Thérèse found another phrase from the words of Jesus to St. Margaret Mary in a prayer book, one of the few books she had at her disposal, entitled *The Little Breviary of the Sacred Heart*: "The cross is the bed of my spouse. It is there where I will have you consume the delights of my love." (Yellow Notebook, August 6, 1897)[17] In the same book she discovered the expression that Jesus used when speaking to St. Margaret Mary, which marked her entire life, "the science of love."[18] St. Thérèse goes on to explain: "Without showing Himself, without making His voice

---

[15] *Letters*, vol. II, p. 709.

[16] *Ibid.*, p. 728.

[17] St. Thérèse of Lisieux, *Last Conversations*, p. 136.

[18] Pope John Paul II chose the expression "The Science of Divine Love" for the title of his Apostolic Letter *Divini Amoris Scientia*, issued on the occasion of the proclamation of the Doctorate of St. Thérèse on October 19, 1997. The Holy Father showed how "Thérèse is a teacher for our times, thirsting for the teachings of Christ and people who witnessed the Gospel message." (*Osservatore Romano*, no 42, October 21, 1997, p. 5).

heard, Jesus teaches me in secret; it is not by means of books, for I do not understand what I am reading. Sometimes a word comes to console me, such as this one, which I received at the end of prayer (after having remained in silence and aridity): 'Here is the teacher whom I am giving you; he will teach you everything that you must do. I want to make you read in the book of life, wherein is contained the science of LOVE.' The science of Love, ah, yes, this word resounds sweetly in the ear of my soul, and I desire only this science" (MsB, 1r).[19]

The Silence of Love

From Samaria to Calvary, from Granada to Parey-le-Monial, from Lisieux to Calcutta, it is always the same cry of Jesus which echoes in the night all over the world. It is always the same thirst of Jesus to be quenched, that same request to His friends to stay awake with Him and pray, to console Him, to carry with Him the sufferings of the world. "I thirst, but with a thirst so burning to be loved by man in the Blessed Sacrament, that this thirst is consuming Me, and I find nobody who would make an effort to meet My desire to quench My thirst and respond to My love."[20] This was before the geniuses of Love arrived, which were St. Margaret Mary, St. Thérèse of Lisieux, Blessed Mother Teresa and we could add others like Marthe Robin. They wanted to respond fully to the love of Jesus by welcoming the flood of tenderness which was stored up in His Merciful Heart.

Blaise Pascal,[21] the great French philosopher wrote: "Jesus

---

[19] *Story of a Soul*, p. 188.

[20] Quoted by Gérard Dufour, *À l'École du Coeur de Jesus avec sainte Marguerite-Marie* [*In the School of the Heart of Jesus with Saint Margaret Mary*. Not translated.], Paris, l'Emmanuel, 1999, p. 86

[21] Blaise Pascal (1623-1662) a mathematical genius, wrote the *Pensées* (*Thoughts*), New York, French & European Publishers, 1991, in which he stated: "If God does not exist, one will lose nothing by believing in him, while if he does exist, one will lose everything by not believing."

will be in agony until the end of time; we must not be asleep during that time." The Catholic French novelist and playwright Georges Bernanos[22] made this the great theme of his entire work. Do we not hear the chants of hate every Good Friday in the songs of lamentation at the Veneration of the Cross while the faithful venerate the stripped Cross? How difficult it is to appreciate and endure our Savior's pain — His love has been so rejected!

> Oh my people what have I done to you?
> In what have I saddened you? Answer me.
> People lost in bitterness,
> People with closed hearts,
> Remember!
> The Master has liberated you.
> So much love; will it be without response?
> So much love of a crucified God?
> I have carried the weight of chains,
> My back bent under the whip
> You hurt me in the oppressed,
> The innocent fallen under the hate
> Oh my brother, answer me.

What can we do to console Jesus and be with Him in His agony which never seems to end, in spite of His Paschal victory? The mystics responded with unanimous voice — we can offer the silence of our love, we can unite in "His loving broken heart" and offer Him through the virtues of the Sacred Heart our life and our freedom. Each one of our daily tasks can become a shelter for Him, a loving home for the "beggar of love" as St. Thérèse modeled for us. Love Him in other people like the Good Samaritan who "showed himself to be a neighbor to the robber's victim" (Lk 10:36).

---

[22] Georges Bernanos (1888-1948) belongs to the French Catholic Literary Revival. His most famous book *Diary of a Country Priest*, shows us that Christ is alive in all suffering of people until the end of times, therefore "all is grace"!

In the words of the novelist Sylvie Germain:[23]

Be present in silence and love like Jesus on the night of Holy Thursday sharing in His powerlessness, and allowing the prayer of Jesus to be prayed in us through the Holy Spirit. Live fully the silence of love, even in faraway countries, by holding on to the empty tabernacle in the dark and soundless night of Holy Thursday. Even if we don't understand anything, we can stay awake with Jesus on the Mount of Olives — the unique mountain where no epiphany happens, no revelation, no transfiguration, but where only total silence is most present.[24]

Germain writes about the vulnerable and undefended God in *The Echoes of Silence* which she dedicated to the seven Trappist monks of Our Lady of Atlas [The Martyrs of Atlas], who were murdered in Algeria in 1996.

God needs those of us who are good like Blessed Mother Teresa, who are committed to saving all people; He needs saints like St. Thérèse who consoled Him by preparing a shelter for Him in the hearts of those who reject Him. Solely purified in the trial of hope alone, those good people and saints have suffered the trial of the dark night of faith, which left them emptied in their depth. They are strangers on this earth, and their heart is in exile. How many Christians are left only to the dynamics of their own wounds, in a world which organizes itself more and more outside of their church?

---

[23] Sylvie Germain, born in 1954, teacher, holds a doctorate in philosophy, one of the foremost novelists and essayists in contemporary France, author of 12 novels, some translated into English [trans.].

[24] Sylvie Germain, *Les Echos du Silence* [*The Echoes of Silence*. Not translated.], Desclée De Brouwer, 1996, p. 35.

They are like the people of Israel exiled in Babylon in the year 587 B.C., scattered all over the Chaldean Empire, called to rediscover their Union with God which was written only in their hearts. Those good people became shepherds also with "broken hearts."

Their most important task will always be to help God, who is helpless, to console the God who is rejected, to find Him new shelter — knowing that the only place where He would agree to stay is in the vast human heart. It is those men and women who are united with God, who strongly identify in the depths of their own shattered selves, that this God suffers also from being rejected by so many of His children who abandon Him, who betray Him, and who are unfaithful to His commandments. They know that however much they love Christ, their love will never be enough to satisfy God's thirst for love which is constantly rejected by the selfishness in the hearts of sinners. Despite their understanding of the painful limitations of mankind, they yearn to share in the incredible joy to love God.[25]

The Dark Night

During the last eighteen months of her life, St. Thérèse of Lisieux suffered in excruciating physical pain as she lay dying from tuberculosis. She also suffered through a dark night of the soul that she called the "night of nothingness."[26] And she went through

---

[25] *Ibid.*, p. 95.

[26] A dark night of the soul in Christian mysticism is a crisis that shakes our deepest conviction about the nature and role in our lives of God, faith, the world and our own personalities. But these dark nights also shake us in our complacency, expose our illusions and false romanticism, show us where we most need God, and invite us to a deeper level of spiritual maturity [trans.].

these struggles all alone. In her last manuscript, she wrote about her tragic confusion, sharing the same table as her unbelieving brothers, so that through her love, faith could grow in them. She quenched the thirst of Jesus by offering Him the gift of her acceptance of being alone in her spiritual darkness and the agony of her physical pain.

> During those very joyful days of the Easter season, Jesus made me feel that there really were souls who have no faith, and who, through the abuse of grace, lost this precious treasure, the source of the only real and pure joy. He permitted my soul to be invaded by the thickest darkness, and that the thought of heaven, up until then so sweet to me, be no longer anything but the cause of struggle and torment... (MsC 5v).[27]
>
> Your child however, O Lord, has understood Your divine light, and she begs pardon for her brothers. She is resigned to eat the bread of sorrow as long as You desire it; she does not wish to rise up from this table filled with bitterness at which poor sinners are eating until the day set by You. Can she not say in her name and in the name of her brothers, "Have pity on us, O Lord, for we are poor sinners!" Oh! Lord, send us away justified. May all those who were not enlightened by the bright flame of faith one day see it shine. O Jesus! If it is needful that the table soiled by them be purified by a soul who loves You, then I desire to eat this bread of trial at this table until it pleases You to bring me into Your bright Kingdom. The only grace I ask of You is that I never offend You! (MsC 6r).[28]
>
> When I want to rest my heart fatigued by the dark-

---

[27] *Story of a Soul*, p. 211.

[28] *Ibid.*, p. 212.

ness that surrounded it by the memory of the luminous country after which I aspire, my torment redoubles; it seems to me that the darkness, borrowing the voice of sinners, says mockingly to me: "You are dreaming about the eternal light, about a fatherland embalmed in the sweetest perfumes; you are dreaming about the eternal possession of the Creator of all these marvels; you believe that one day you will walk out of this fog that surrounds you! Advance, advance; rejoice in death which will give you not what you hope for but a night still more profound, the night of nothingness" (MsC 6v).[29]

I tell Him, too, I am happy not to enjoy this beautiful heaven on this earth so that He will open it for all eternity to poor unbelievers. Also, in spite of this trial which has taken away all my joy, I can nevertheless cry out: "You have given me DELIGHT, O Lord, in ALL your doings." For is there a joy greater than that of suffering out of love for You? The more interior the suffering is and the less apparent to the eyes of creatures, the more it rejoices You, O my God! But if my suffering was really unknown to You, which is impossible, I would still be happy to have it, if through it I could prevent or make reparation for one single sin against faith (MsC 7r).[30]

The Loss of God

Blessed Mother Teresa also realized the tragic silence of God. She had lived through the harsh realities of the twentieth century

---

[29] *Ibid.*, p. 213.
[30] *Ibid.*, p. 214.

by feeling solidarity with the victims of evil who search in darkness for a light, a hope, and a meaning. Her loving presence showed us how she felt the suffering of a God, wounded by so much fanaticism and indifference. Like St. Thérèse, she had quenched Jesus' thirst for love and the thirst for love of His children by becoming herself a victim of love. She accomplished this by being faithful in the little things and by allowing herself to be drawn by Jesus' suffering love thus becoming part of His cry on the cross: "My God, my God why have you forsaken me?" (Mt 45:46).

When Blessed Mother Teresa's personal journal is finally published, the surprise will be great. We will learn that she had lived her faith through a tormenting trial afflicted with excruciating and painful doubt about the existence of God. This dark night became her daily suffering for most of her life. She confided in her journal: "The people damned in hell suffer an eternal punishment because they experience the loss of God. In my soul I feel the terrible pain of that loss. I feel that God does not want me, that He is not God and that He does not really exist."[31]

In his Second Lenten Conference of 2003 at the Cathedral of Notre Dame in Paris, Cardinal Paul Poupard also quoted from Blessed Mother Teresa's writings about the complete spiritual darkness in her life:

> "My smile is a great mantle which covers a multitude of sufferings," she wrote in July of 1958. "I smile all the time. The sisters and people think that my faith, my hope and my love are profoundly fulfilling me, and that intimacy with God and union with His will, live in my heart. If they only knew... only blind faith moves me along, because the truth is that all is darkness for me. Sometimes the agony of desolation is so great and at

---

[31] Quoted by Bruce Johnston, in the journal *Ottawa Citizen*, November 29, 2002, p. 8.

the same time the living hope for The Absent so profound, that the only prayer I am able to recite is: 'Sacred Heart of Jesus I place all my trust in You. I will
quench your thirst for souls.'"[32]

Blessed Mother Teresa experienced the pain of the lone
shepherd [referring to the poem of St. John of the Cross cited on
page 61], as a suffering caused by the indifference of His shepherdess who rejected His love. Blessed Mother Teresa's dark night
of faith became like Jesus' death on the cross, a night of love. In
suffering like Jesus from feeling unloved, she dressed her wounds
by giving herself to the poorest of the poor. Nevertheless she always acted as if God loved her, even if she did not feel this love
and doubted its existence. Yet her blind faith in God brought her
to deep personal prayer. She suffered from desiring Jesus, and
wanting to share in His thirst. And, at the same time, she felt the
pain of people who were rejected and unloved.

This darkness of faith and hope made her share in the skepticism of a society which put religion aside especially in the Western world. In order to resist the pain of darkness she doubled her
love. Her actions were enormously fruitful resulting from the great
dryness in the time she spent in prayer. Her words emerged from
absolute silence, like those who are completely filled with the Holy
Spirit and worship in silence and in truth. Marked by total silence
and a dark night of faith, Mother Teresa welcomed the wound of
the Good Shepherd.

The contemplatives and the ascetics of all ages and re-
ligions have always sought God in the silence and solitude of the desert, forests, and mountains. Jesus Himself spent forty days in the desert and the mountains,
communicating for long hours with the Father in the

---

[32] Cardinal Paul Poupard, *La Sainteté au défi de l'Histoire* [*Sainthood in Defiance of History.*
Not translated.], Presses de la Renaissance, Paris, 2003, p. 82.

silence of the night. We, too, are called to withdraw at certain intervals into deeper silence and aloneness with God, together as a community as well as personally. To be alone with Him, not with our books, thoughts, and memories but completely stripped of everything, to dwell lovingly in His presence — silent, empty, expectant and motionless.[33]

The Gift of Joy

St. John of the Cross has shown with great eloquence that the dark night in Christian understanding, is a night of love and joy. This night is a lived experience with Christ who died and was risen and became present in the absence. We often feel His love as an absence, but Jesus allows us to rejoice in His presence in faith. When we feel the absence of someone who is dear to us, we want that person to be present because they are present in our heart. This absence increases our desire and we feel even more distant, which increases our yearning for closeness. Simone Weil,[34] the great French philosopher asked if God is present only in the form of absence.

The shepherdess in the poem of St. John of the Cross does not remember that presence in the absence. She forgot her shepherd and no longer enjoyed His presence. Her heart was in a different place. She no longer was the shelter for her friend although the heart of the shepherd was all hers. He wanted to draw her to Himself and take her "with human attachments and bonds of love" (*Spiritual Works* 11,4). He suffered like all of us when we don't feel our love is reciprocated and He also suffered for His friend

---

[33] Mother Teresa, *No Greater Love...*, p. 9.

[34] Simone Weil (1909-1943). A modern religious intellect and mystic noted for her uncompromising search for the truth of our God. T.S. Eliot described her as "a woman of genius, a kind of genius akin to that of the saints." [trans.]

who moved in a different direction without His love. If she only knew what it meant to be loved by such a friend… but how could the shepherd demonstrate His love to her?

He climbed a tree, opened His arms and remained there hanging, "His loving heart broken." He died attached to the tree. A sublime image of the cross! Having loved until the very end, the lone shepherd died of love for her by giving His life; He also died through her because she refused His love. "I have come to call not the righteous but to bring sinners to repentance" (Lk 5:32). He died forgiving, because we did not know what we were doing. He died, His heart pierced by a lance so that His heart could heal us once and for all and reveal to us the Father. He was the Divine Physician who came for the sick. And, by His cross, earth was lit with His fire and we were able to reach for heaven. Thus, this tree of life opens Paradise for us. Everything was given to us at the foot of the Cross: a mother, pardon, thirst, and a heart. "And I, when I am lifted up from the earth, will draw all people to myself" (Jn 12:32).

The depth of Jesus' heart will reveal itself in the secret of the wound, His open side which will not close anymore; it will stay open because we are to understand that love is infinite, beyond anything that suffering can show. The testimony of St. Catherine of Siena, Doctor of the Church[35] puts it beautifully when she asked Jesus why He wanted to have His heart opened, since He was already dead. He responded:

> Because my desire towards every person was infinite and the real work of enduring pain was finished. But because the work was finished, I could not show all the love which I have for you, because my love has no end and is never finished. That is why I wanted you to see

---

[35] Out of thirty-three in the history of the Church, there are three female saints who have been proclaimed a Doctor of the Church: St. Catherine of Siena, St. Teresa of Avila and St. Thérèse of Lisieux.

the secret of My Heart and show it to you open, so that you see that I loved you more than any work of finite suffering can show.[36]

We were born of this wound of the Lamb from which blood gushed forth, and the blood and water were merged for weddings not only at Cana but all times. As with St. Catherine of Siena and St. Margaret Mary, the Merciful Heart was once again revealed to another young woman, as late as between the two World Wars, St. Faustina Kowalska. She became the first woman canonized by Pope John Paul II during the Jubilee Year 2000. He announced that the first Sunday after Easter would be called from then on "Divine Mercy Sunday," responding to the desire Jesus Himself had revealed on February 22, 1931, to this simple Polish religious of twenty-five years. Love never ceases to spend itself.

St. John of the Cross told us that by approaching the love of the Heart of Jesus, it becomes possible for us to empty ourselves completely so that we can make room for Him. From the emptied self of our mortal humanity surges the "all" of the fullness of God, who only waits for our empty self to be offered freely. This heart which initially searches for us first begs our "yes" and does not want to be forgotten. He graces us with love for Him so that we might allow Him to find us. He set the promised day to come again at the end of times, and offers us today a life in His future by way of abandonment and confidence.

St. Thérèse wrote a poem entitled *To The Sacred Heart of Jesus* in which the risen Jesus Himself was the beloved person. She had the same fire burning within her as did her great spiritual brother St. John of the Cross. Once again her focus is on the "science of love" lived out as a relational work of love, which is the essence of her teaching. Rarely has she expressed it as clearly as in the following poem:

---

[36] Catherine of Siena, *The Dialogue,* translation and introduction by Suzanne Noffke, O.P., Paulist Press, Mahwah, NJ, 1988, p. 133.

To the Sacred Heart of Jesus

"I need a heart burning with tenderness,
Who will be my support forever,
Who loves everything in me, even my weakness...
And who never leaves me day or night."
I could find no creature
Who could always love me and never die.
I must have a God who takes on my nature
And becomes my brother and is able to suffer!
You heard me, only Friend whom I love.
To ravish my heart, you become man.
You shed your blood, what a supreme mystery!...
And you still live for me on the Altar.
If I cannot see the brilliance of your Face
Or hear your sweet voice,
O my God, I can live by your grace,
I can rest on your Sacred Heart!
O Heart of Jesus, treasure of tenderness,
You Yourself are my happiness, my only hope.
You who knew how to charm my tender youth,
Stay near me till the last night.
Lord, to you alone I've given my life,
And all my desires are well-known to you.
It's in your ever-infinite goodness
That I want to lose myself, O Heart of Jesus! (PN 23)[37]

---

[37] *The Poetry of Saint Thérèse of Lisieux*, translated by Donald Kinney, O.C.D., ICS Publications, Washington, DC, p. 120.

The Holy Trinity as the Fire of Love

The Good News of God's love revealed in Jesus is not exclusively ours. Every disciple, namely each one of us, is called to spread it all over the world. It was a great desire of the Sacred Heart of Jesus to ignite this fire of love everywhere: "I have come to bring fire to the earth and how I wish it were already kindled" (Lk 13:49). It was to be spread by Jesus' first disciples, who were inspired by the fire of the Holy Spirit to proclaim the Word in all languages: "Divided tongues, as of fire, appeared among them, and a tongue rested on each of them" (Ac 2:3). It is no longer Moses who was set ablaze by the burning bush through the "I AM," but the friends of the Lamb who became exhilarated by the Spirit because they were taken by a burning embrace, that of the Father and the Son and the Holy Spirit.

The fire which was at first ignited on the Cross, burst forth from the empty tomb and blazed through the disciples on Pentecost so as to flow from person to person and from generation to generation. "No one after lighting a lamp puts it under the bushel basket, but on the lamp stand, and it gives light to all in the house" (Mt 5:15). Paul of Tarsus was blinded by it on the way to Damascus. This fire became an immense blaze with uncountable martyrs and Church Fathers, long lines of hermits and monks, thousands of religious founders and mystics, and a constant stream of fathers and mothers who transform their family and homes into furnaces of love for the world. Christian hope spreads like a growing fire over the entire creation lighting up caves, houses, villages, countrysides, deserts and forests; enlightening children and kings, poets and musicians, philosophers and scientists, the poor and the rich.

St. Thérèse and Blessed Mother Teresa, two women on fire, who died a century apart, wanted to spread their desire for Jesus and quench His thirst for love. In her poem entitled *Jesus, My Beloved, Remember!* (stanza 17), St. Thérèse, Patroness of the Missions, wrote about this wish to carry the fire of God to the four corners of the world — which has become reality today through the visit of her relics throughout the world:

> One weak spark, O mystery of life,
> Is enough to light a huge fire,
> That I want, O my God,
> To carry your Fire far and wide,
> Remember (PN 24).[1]

The Lever of Prayer

Blessed Mother Teresa, a woman of great desire, lived her life in prayer and adoration. In her echoed the biblical words: "Let everyone who is thirsty come. Let anyone who wishes, take the water of life as a gift" (Rv 22:17). She herself drew from the living water especially in the evening with her sisters during their hour of Eucharistic Adoration. Blessed Mother Teresa reflected:

> Every evening, when we return from our work we come together in our chapel for an hour of continuous adoration. In the stillness of the moment of the setting sun,

---

[1] *The Poetry of Saint Thérèse of Lisieux,* p. 127.

we find peace in the presence of Christ. This hour of intimacy with Jesus is crucial. I saw a great transformation accomplished in our congregation ever since the day we established the practice of daily adoration. Our love for Jesus has become more familiar, more integrated as part of the family and has increased the love that we have for one another. Our love for the sick has become more compassionate.[2]

The transformation through adoration of the Holy Eucharist, that Mother Teresa described here, we have also observed in the parishes and the young religious movements where Eucharistic Adoration has been reinstated. More and more the Blessed Sacrament is being exposed on the altars all over the world not only in the new religious communities and pilgrim sites — Lourdes, Lisieux, and Fatima — but in the simple chapels of perpetual adoration in parishes in every diocese. By commitment to a continual presence, hundreds of people take turns in Eucharistic prayer, day and night. The silent prayer supports the work of evangelization of the parish cells. Those who pray in adoration before the Blessed Sacrament try to reconnect themselves to the Source, deeply inspired by the Good Samaritan, in order to better proclaim the Good News of salvation.

The work of evangelization begins with hours of silent adoration before the Blessed Sacrament where believers relive the death and resurrection of Christ and commune with His Heart overflowing with love: "I thirst." Each person goes forth to act as a link in the chain of vessels sharing the overflow of God's love and imitating the life of Christ in the Gospel. Evangelization has its place in the mystery of the Eucharist, "the summit to which all action of the Church is directed and at the same time the source from whence all its virtue comes" (Vatican II, *Constitution on the*

---

2   Mother Teresa, *No Greater Love...*, p. 154.

Sacred Liturgy, 10). If this occurs what we will see is the weaving of a new fabric growing from an interconnection of small parish cells with a mission totally focused on evangelization all over the world. People's commitment to the faith will become more active and this will produce works of genuine compassion.[3]

Blessed Mother Teresa often said that the time spent in front of the Blessed Sacrament is the greatest treasure of the Missionaries of Charity. St. Thérèse said the same about prayer:

> A scholar has said: 'Give me a lever and a fulcrum and I will lift the world.' What Archimedes was not able to obtain, for his request was not directed to God and was only made from a material viewpoint, the saints have obtained in all its fullness. The Almighty has given them as fulcrum: HIMSELF ALONE; as lever: PRAYER which burns with a fire of love. It is in this way that they have lifted the world; it is in this way that the saints still militantly lift it, and that, until the end of time, the saints to come will lift it (MsC 36r-36v).[4]

For the two Theresas, the time spent in silent prayer was most often in aridity, and became a privileged occasion to unite with the "I thirst" of Jesus, He who suffers from often being forgotten by His brothers and sisters. It was also a time to rest their hearts in the Heart of Jesus and return love for love to Him. St. Thérèse wrote these words to her sister Céline, which could have very well been addressed to Blessed Mother Teresa:

> Céline, since Jesus was "alone in treading the wine" which He is giving us to drink, let us not refuse in our

---

[3]   *Oïkos-Evangelization*, a Canadian movement, distributes *The Paraclete*, a bulletin for the liaison of parish cells of evangelization. In June of 2003, the 14th International Colloquium on the system of parish cells of evangelization, was held at Milan, Italy.

[4]   *Story of a Soul*, p. 258.

turn to wear clothing stained in blood... let us tread for Jesus a new wine, which may quench His thirst, which will return Him love for love. Ah, let us not keep back one drop of wine that we can offer Him... and then, looking about, He will see that we are coming to help Him!... let us make a little tabernacle in our heart where Jesus may take refuge, and then He will be consoled, and He will forget what we cannot forget: the ingratitude of souls that abandon Him in a deserted tabernacle!... forgetfulness, it seems to me that it is this which causes Him the greatest sorrow! (LT 108).[5]

St. Thérèse knew that suffering was the place where the call to share in the thirst of Christ who transforms our broken selves into fire can be heard the loudest. This does not mean that we must suffer joyfully: "I have found the secret of suffering in peace... the one who says *peace* is not saying *joy*, or at least, *felt joy*.... To suffer in peace it is enough to will all that Jesus wills..."(LT 87).[6] She pointed out to us that we should look at the Holy Face and understand suffering as a part of the human condition, which for her was so significant that she even added this holy reference to her religious name, St. Thérèse of the Child Jesus and the Holy Face: "Jesus is on fire with love for us.... Look at His adorable Face! Look at His eyes lifeless and lowered! Look at His wounds.... There you will see how He loves us" (LT 87). It is there, in the image of Love hidden in His suffering expression, were we can find the Divine, humbling Himself, and reaching down to us in a gift of total giving even in accepting a violent death. By His death on the Cross, He revealed the secret of His heart, which He offers to us in the sacred wounds of His resurrected body.

---

[5]   *Letters of Saint Thérèse of Lisieux*, vol. I, p. 630.
[6]   *Ibid.*, p. 553.

The Prisoner of Love

During the hours of adoration in the chapel, St. Thérèse and Blessed Mother Teresa wanted to console Jesus and redoubled their efforts in their own dark nights of spiritual struggle. It seems challenging for us to understand that it is especially in those times of inner darkness, that Jesus, being our prisoner within us, communicates most profoundly His thirst for souls: "Give me to drink." At the inner well of their own desert, when they experienced a total feeling of aridity, they thrust themselves into the depth of Jesus' Heart and united with Him. Then, receiving the hidden God and fortified with His overflowing love, they immediately gave Him to those in greatest need and most suffering in Carmel and in Calcutta. They had touched Jesus, the Son of God by serving others. Both of these women had hearts full of love yet broken, but they relentlessly placed themselves like magnets on the open heart of Jesus on the Cross, and the great God became forever a prisoner in them and they in Him, day and night, rooted in Him forever for His joy, for theirs and ours. "How great must a soul be to contain a God" (LT 165).[7] St. Thérèse in her poem *The Canticle of Sister Marie of the Trinity and of the Holy Face*, expresses the most intimate relationship between Jesus and ourselves in the image of the prisoner of love:

> You, the Great God whom all Heaven adores,
> You live in me, my Prisoner night and day.
> Constantly your sweet voice implores me.
> You repeat: "I thirst... I thirst for Love!..."
> I am also your prisoner,
> And I want in turn to repeat
> Your tender, divine prayer:
> "My Beloved, My Brother,

---

[7] *Letters*, vol. II, p. 863.

I thirst for Love!..."
I thirst for Love, fulfill my hope.
Lord, make your Divine Fire grow within me.
I thirst for Love, so great is my suffering.
Ah! I would like to fly away to you, my God!...
Your love is my only martyrdom.
The more I feel it burning within me,
The more my soul desires You....
    Jesus, make me die
        Of Love for You!!!... (PN 31).[8]

---

[8]   *The Poetry of Saint Thérèse of Lisieux*, p. 151.

Act of Oblation to Merciful Love

O My God! Most Blessed Trinity, I desire to Love You and make You Loved, to work for the glory of Holy Church by saving souls on earth and liberating those suffering in purgatory. I desire to accomplish Your will perfectly and to reach the degree of glory You have prepared for me in Your Kingdom. I desire, in a word, to be a Saint, but I feel my helplessness and I beg You, O my God! To be Yourself my Sanctity!

Since You loved me so much as to give me Your only Son as my Savior and my Spouse, the infinite treasures of His merits are mine. I offer them to You with gladness, begging You to look upon me only in the Face of Jesus and His Heart burning with Love.

I offer You, too, all the merits of the saints (in heaven and on earth), their acts of Love, and those of the holy angels. Finally, I offer You, O Blessed Trinity! the Love and merits of the Blessed Virgin, my dear Mother. It is to her I abandon my offering, begging her to present it to You. Her Divine Son, my Beloved Spouse, told us in the days of His mortal life: "Whatsoever you ask the Father in My name He will give it to you!" I am certain, then, that You will grant my desires; I know, O my God! that the more You want to give, the more You make us desire. I feel in my heart immense desires and it is with confidence I ask You to come and take possession of my soul. Ah! I cannot receive Holy Communion as often as I desire, but, Lord, are You not all-powerful? Remain in me as in a tabernacle and never separate Yourself from Your little victim.

I want to console You for the ingratitude of the wicked, and I beg of You to take away my freedom to displease You. If through weakness I sometimes fall, may Your Divine Glance cleanse my soul immediately, consuming all my imperfections like the fire that transforms everything into itself.

I thank You, O my God! for all the graces You have granted me, especially the grace of making me pass through the crucible of suffering. It is with joy I shall contemplate You on the Last Day carrying the scepter of Your Cross. Since You deigned to give me a share in this very precious Cross, I hope in heaven to resemble You and to see shining in my glorified body the sacred stigmata of Your Passion.

After earth's Exile, I hope to go and enjoy You in the Fatherland, but I do not want to lay up merits for heaven. I want to work for Your Love alone with the one purpose of pleasing You, consoling Your Sacred Heart, and saving souls who will love You eternally.

In the evening of this life, I shall appear before You with empty hands, for I do not ask You, Lord, to count my works. All our justice is stained in Your eyes. I wish, then, to be clothed in Your own Justice and to receive from Your Love the eternal possession of Yourself. I want no other Throne, no other Crown but You, my Beloved!

Time is nothing in Your eyes, and a single day is like a thousand years. You can, then, in one instant prepare me to appear before You.

In order to live in one single act of perfect Love, I OFFER MYSELF AS A VICTIM OF HOLOCAUST TO YOUR MERCIFUL LOVE, asking You to consume me incessantly, allowing the waves of infinite tenderness shut up within You to overflow into my soul, and that thus I may become a martyr of Your Love, O my God!

May this martyrdom, after having prepared me to appear before You, finally cause me to die and may my soul take its flight without any delay into the eternal embrace of Your Merciful Love.

I want, O my Beloved, at each beat of my heart to renew this offering to You an infinite number of times, until the shadows having disappeared I may be able to tell You of my Love in an Eternal Face to Face!

Marie-Françoise-Thérèse of the Child Jesus
and the Holy Face, unworthy Carmelite religious

This 9th day of June,
Feast of the Most Holy Trinity
In the year of grace 1895

Spiritual Testament of Mother Teresa

My children, my dear Sisters, Brothers and Fathers, since this letter is very personal, I wanted to write it with my own hand but there are so many things to say.... But even if they are not from my hand, they come from my heart!

Jesus wants that I tell you — especially in this Holy Week — how much love He has for each one of you, beyond all you can imagine. I worry that some of you have not really met Jesus — one on one: you and Jesus alone. We can certainly spend time in the chapel, but have you perceived — with the eyes of the soul — with what love He looks at you? Have you really come to know the living Jesus, not from books but by offering Him shelter in your hearts? Have you heard His words of love? Ask for this grace; He has the burning desire to give it to you. As long as you do not hear Jesus in the silence of your heart, you can not hear Him say "I thirst" in the heart of your poor ones. Never abandon the intimate daily contact with Jesus as a real and living person, instead of just a pure idea. How can we spend even one single day without listening to Jesus when He says: "I love you." (...) That is impossible! Our soul needs that as much as our body needs to breathe. If not, prayer dies and meditation degenerates into simple reflection. Jesus wants that each one of us listen to Him, as He speaks to you in the silence of your heart. Be attentive to what could prevent this personal contact with the living Jesus. The devil will try to use the wounds of life, indeed our very own faults, in order to persuade you that it is impossible for Jesus to really love you. Beware, that this is a danger for all of us. But the saddest thing is, that this is completely contrary to what Jesus would want and expect to hear from you. Not only that He loves you but even more; He ardently desires you. He misses you when you do not come close to Him. He is thirsty for you. He loves you always even when you do not feel worthy of Him. When you are not accepted by others — or even sometimes by yourself — He always accepts you.

My children, you don't have to be different (from what you are in reality) for Jesus to love you. Believe simply that you are precious to Him. Bring your sufferings to His feet and simply open your heart so that He loves you the way you are, and He will do the rest. Each one of you is aware that Jesus loves you but with this letter I want to address your heart. Jesus desires to move our hearts so as not to lose our first love [our vocation], especially in the future when I will have left you. This is why I want you to read this letter in front of the Blessed Sacrament, in the place where it was written so that Jesus Himself can speak to each one of you. Why do I tell you this? The letter of the Holy Father about "I thirst" struck me so much that it is hard for me to tell you what I felt. This letter has allowed me to discover even more the beauty of our vocation. How great is God's love for us because He has chosen our congregation to quench this Thirst of Jesus — His thirst for love, and thirst for souls — by giving us a special place in His Church.

At the same time, we remind the world of that thirst which is about to be forgotten. I wrote to the Holy Father to thank him. His letter[1] is a sign of that "great thirst" that Jesus experiences for

---

[1]   On this theme, see Pope John Paul II's Letter to Sister Nirmala Joshi, "Continue to Quench Christ's Thirst for Souls" on the occasion of the 50th Anniversary of the Missionaries of Charity - 2 October 2000, in *L'Osservatore Romano*, N. 43 - 25 October 2000, p. 6. See also http://www.catholic-forum.com/saints/pope0264gh.htm

each human being. It is also a sign for me, a sign that the time has come to speak openly about the gift given to me on September 10, to explain — as well as I can — what the Thirst of Jesus means for me. For me the Thirst of Jesus is something so intimate that until now my shyness prevented me from talking to you about what happened on September 10. At first, I thought I should imitate Our Lady who "kept all those things in her heart." That is why I have not talked about "I thirst," particularly in public. Nevertheless my letters and instructions always pointed it out, and showed the means to quench this thirst through prayer, intimacy with Jesus and respect for our vows, especially the fourth one. For me it is very clear that everything about the Missionaries of Charity (M.C.) is intended to quench the Thirst of Jesus. His words, written on the walls of all the chapels of the M.C.'s, are not of the past but living, here and now spoken to you. Do you believe in them? If yes, you would hear and feel His presence. Let Him become as intimate to you as He is in me. That would be the greatest joy that you could offer me. I will try to help you understand those words, but it is Jesus Himself who alone can tell you "I thirst!" Hear your own name being called, and not only one time — but every day. When you listen with your heart you will hear, you will understand. Why did Jesus cry out, "I thirst"? How do we have to understand it? It is very difficult to explain with words… and yet, if you would retain one thing from this letter, it should be this: "I thirst" is a much deeper phrase than if Jesus would have just said, "I love you." As long as you do not know in a very intimate way that Jesus is thirsty for you, it will be impossible for you to know who He wants to be for you, nor who He wants you to be for Him. The heart and the soul of the M.C. consists exclusively in — the Thirst in the Heart of Jesus hidden in the poor. This is the only source from which the life of the M.C. is nourished and it shows you our goal as well as our fourth vow and the spirit of our congregation. To quench the Thirst of the living Jesus among us, is the only reason for this congregation to exist and is its unique objective. Tell me, can we say about ourselves as well, that we know this is our only reason to live? In order to know it ask yourself the following question: suppose that the Thirst of Jesus be no longer our goal and be no longer written on the walls of our chapels, would that bring about a difference in my vocation and in my relation with Jesus and in my work? Would it change anything in my life, and would I feel a big loss? Ask yourselves these questions honestly and let them be for everyone the test to discover whether the Thirst of Jesus is a living reality in his/her life and not only a beautiful idea.... "I thirst" (Jn 19:28) and "You have done it to me" (Mt 25:30): remember that you must always combine these two phrases, the means with the goal. Let no one separate what God has united.

Let us not underestimate our very concrete means — work for the poor, however small or humble it is — which makes something very beautiful out of our lives in the eyes of the Lord. Those are the most precious gifts from God to our congregation. Because of this presence of Jesus, so hidden and yet so near, He is able to touch us.

In our work for the poor, our goal would disappear and the Thirst of Jesus would reduce itself to words, empty of meaning and response. But by uniting the two, our missionary vocation will remain living and real, just as Our Lady requested.

Be also judicious in the choice of those who preach our retreats. Not everyone understands our spirit well. Even if they were wise men and saints, it would still not guarantee that they necessarily understand our vocation. Besides, if they came to tell you something different from what I have written in this letter, I beg you not to listen to them or let them confuse you. The Thirst of Jesus is the source, the focus, and the goal of everything the Missionaries of Charity are and do. The Church has confirmed it several times: "Our call is to quench the Thirst of Jesus, the Thirst for love of souls by working for the salvation and the sanctification of the poorest of the poor." That and only that, nothing else.

Let us do everything in our power to protect the gift of God to our congregation.

Dear children, have confidence in me and listen to me attentively to what I tell you now:

Only the Thirst of Jesus together with our constant listening, our search, and our heartfelt response, only that Thirst will keep our congregation alive after I will have left you. If this Thirst is truly made the basis of your life, everything will go well for us. One day I will have left you, but the Thirst of Jesus will never leave you. The thirsting Jesus in the poor, you will have with you always. For that reason I want the active Sisters and the active Brothers, the contemplative Sisters with the Brothers and Priests to help each other mutually to nourish Jesus (to quench His Thirst) with the means of their respective gifts: by supporting each other, sharing with one another; you are one family united in this one goal and that unique objective.

Do not exclude Cooperators or the lay Missionaries from that requirement but help them to understand it, because that vocation is also theirs. Since the first task of the priest is the ministry of preaching, I have asked our priests several years ago to start preaching on that theme: "I thirst!" in order to enter deeper into the gift that God granted us on September 10. And since I feel clearly that Jesus will ask them in the future to preach more and more on this subject, pray to Our Lady to keep them focused on that important aspect of their fourth vow. Our Lady will help us all to remain faithful because it was she, who — with St. John and I am sure St. Mary Magdalene — was the first person to hear the cry of Jesus: "I thirst!"

Since she has been at Calvary, she knows the intensity and the depth of this ardent desire of Jesus for us and for the poor. But the rest of us, do we know it…? Do we feel it as she did? Ask her to teach you because you and the whole congregation are hers. Her mission is to bring you to see the love in the Heart of the Crucified Jesus as she did for St. John and St. Mary Magdalene.

Previously Our Lady asked me but now it is I who ask you in her name, begging you: "Hear the Thirst of Jesus." May it be for each one as the Holy Father expressed in his letter: a Gospel for Life.

How do you approach the Thirst of Jesus? One single secret: the closer you come to Jesus, the better you come to know His Thirst. "Repent and believe in the Gospel," Jesus said to us. Of what should we repent? Our indifference, our hardness of heart. And what should we believe in? That Jesus is Thirsty, from now on for your heart and for the poor. He who knows your weakness, desires nevertheless only your love: He simply wants you to let Him love you. He is the master of time, and each time when we approach Him, He associates us with Our Lady, St. John, and St. Mary Magdalene.

Listen to Him. Listen as He calls your very own name.

Thus will my joy and yours be complete.

Pray. And God will bless you.

Mother Teresa

An Interview with Father Brian Kolodiejchuk, M.C., Postulator of the Cause for the Beatification of Mother Teresa

Interviewer: Mother Teresa impressed the world by her dedication to the poorest of the poor. How was it possible for a frail woman to go out into the streets of Calcutta and the world to cure the sores of lepers and caress the "pariahs" of modern societies?

Fr. Brian: I think the key to her life is, precisely, the fact that she was a woman totally in love with Jesus. We have found writings from the time of her youth in which she said that Jesus was her first love. She spoke as a girl who was in love.

For her, her dedication to the neediest, to the poorest of the poor, was the response to a call. Even in moments of darkness, she was convinced that it was an authentic call from Jesus. She was convinced of that phrase that she often repeated: "God's work." She felt like God's pen, his instrument.

Interviewer: Every beatification is a message for the world. What is the message the Church is giving in announcing Mother Teresa's beatification?

Fr. Brian: Her central message is love: toward God, not just toward her neighbor.

At the time that she felt the call to found the congregation of the Missionaries of Charity, she experienced a harsh interior trial; it was a spiritual experience in which she did not feel consolation. However, also in these times of trial, it was love that led her to respond to her mission.

On one occasion, in giving her public recognition, India's Prime Minister Indira Gandhi said these words more or less: "In this world of today, so frenetic, it is easy to forget the most essential things. Mother Teresa teaches us that love is what is most essential."

At the same time, her life is full of examples of love for others, not just for the poor, but also for all persons whom she met: the sister Missionaries of Charity, the people who visited her. In reality, Mother Teresa leaves us the message to do ordinary things with extraordinary love.

When she spoke to the people she met, she said that this attitude should not just be lived with the poor: one must begin by loving the members of one's family who are in need of a word of encouragement. One must begin by loving someone one knows who might be in need of a letter, one must begin to love by giving a smile to the needy.

However, we have been able to see how faith is also one of her characteristic virtues, because otherwise one cannot love in that way, from morning till night, sleeping three or four hours at night, giving herself each day of her life to the neediest.

Interviewer: What has been the greatest challenge of the process of beatification?

Fr. Brian: There were two particularly difficult tasks.

The first, to collect or find all the available information, because it meant collecting material, testimonies, facts coming from people all over the world. In the process, we have compiled more than 8,000 documents, 80 volumes of documentation with testimonies and writings.

In the process, there have been testimonies of 113 persons on her life, virtue and fame for holiness. However, hundreds of other people, being unable to travel, have sent their testimony. We have not been satisfied to do only the indispensable work. We have done much more than the minimum, because this work has served to understand her person better.

The second challenge was the writing of the "positio," the document in which all the testimonies, deeds, documents are recorded on which to base the postulation of her cause of beatification. As there was so much material, it wasn't at all easy. We have been able to count on a really good team, made up of priests, women religious and lay people, volunteers, who made all this work possible.

Interviewer: Have you discovered aspects of Mother Teresa that were hidden when you carried out this huge research?

Fr. Brian: We have been able to understand that her simplicity concealed in reality a depth that very few had understood or even imagined.

When she started the Missionaries of Charity, at 36, she demonstrates in her writings an amazing spiritual maturity. We knew that a person with this worldwide reputation for holiness and the extraordinary attraction she exercised had to have something. But, what was it? This was her secret. Her depth, her spiritual life, her love even in trials — are now exposed.

Interviewer: In recent months there has been talk of the "dark night" that, like the mystics, Mother Teresa felt in important periods of her life. What did it consist of?

Fr. Brian: Spiritual fruit comes from sacrifice, from the cross. Prior to the inspiration for her work, she had already had an experience of darkness. However, it is important to keep in mind that this "night," this inner suffering, is the fruit of her union with Christ, as happened with St. Teresa of Jesus, or Paul of the Cross.

On one side is union with Jesus and love unites. And, being united to Christ, she understood Christ's suffering when he cried from the cross: "My God, my God why hast thou abandoned me?"

However, this "night," this suffering, is also caused by the apostolate, the love of others. Loving Christ, she also understands the suffering of others, their loneliness, and also their distancing of themselves from God.

Mother Teresa's "dark night" was due, therefore, to the double dimension that the love of men and women religious experiences: in the first place, the "spousal," her love of Christ, which leads her to be united to his sufferings and, in the second place, the "redemptive" love, which leads to sharing in the redemption, to proclaim to others the love of God so that they will discover salvation through prayer and sacrifice.

Therefore, more than a test of faith, it was a test of love. More than suffering from the experience of not feeling the love of Jesus, she suffered because of her desire for Jesus, her thirst for Jesus, her thirst for love. The goal of the congregation is, precisely, to slake the thirst of Jesus on the cross through our love for him and our dedication to souls.

Mother not only shared physical and material poverty with the poor, she felt the thirst, the abandonment that people experience. In fact, the greatest poverty is not to be loved, to be rejected.

Interviewer: Some newspapers or news agencies have tried to deny the miraculous character of the cure that has opened the doors of the process of the beatification of Mother Teresa of Calcutta. What is the real story?

Fr. Brian: It is the case of an Indian woman, Monika Besra, who was cured on Sept. 5, 1998, the first anniversary of Mother Teresa's death.

On one hand, she suffered from tubercular meningitis. On the other, she had a large abdominal cystic mass that originated in her right ovary. This large cystic mass disappeared without any medical explanation, as the scientific commission verified that analyzed the case.

It is true that the tubercular meningitis could have been cured, as some newspapers have said, by the effect of medicine. However, this wasn't the miracle. The miracle was the sudden — in one night — and inexplicable cure from the tumefaction.

December 20, 2002 [1]

---

[1]   See www.cin.org/archives/cinjub2002 12/0138.html-14k.

Lord, When I Am Hungry

Lord,
When I am hungry,
Give me someone who needs food.
When I am thirsty,
Send me someone who needs water.
When I am cold,
Send me someone who needs to warm up.
When I am hurt,
Send me someone to be consoled.

When my cross becomes heavy,
Give me the cross of someone else to share.
When I am poor,
Guide me to someone who is in need.
When I have no time,
Send me someone who I can help for a moment.
When I am humiliated,
Give me someone who I can praise.
When I am discouraged,
Send me someone to encourage.
When I need to understand others,
Send me someone who needs my understanding.
When I need help for myself,
Send me someone for whom I can care.
When I only think of myself,
Turn my thoughts to others.

Mother Teresa

ST PAULS

This book was produced by St. Pauls/Alba House, the Society of St. Paul, an international religious congregation of priests and brothers dedicated to serving the Church through the communications media.

For information regarding this and associated ministries of the Pauline Family of Congregations, write to the Vocation Director, Society of St. Paul, P.O. Box 189, 9531 Akron-Canfield Road, Canfield, Ohio 44406-0189. Phone (330) 702-0359; or E-mail: spvocationoffice@aol.com or check our internet site, www.albahouse.org